Welcome to
The Minecraft Book

The popularity of Minecraft is as vast as the world you have to explore within the game. Since its release in 2009, it has won over players of all ages with its colourful landscapes, amusing characters and endless possibilities. Starting from the moment you're dropped into your newly created world, we'll walk you through everything you need to know to survive and thrive in Minecraft. Learn how to construct your first shelter, mine coal and minerals and start growing your own crops, all with our step-by-step guides. Understand everything about the game worlds, mobs and resources on offer, and take things to the next level with our extensive guide to using redstone and constructing elaborate circuits. We'll also show you how to apply texture packs, challenge others players and defeat the Ender Dragon. And to finish it off, at the back of the book the reference guide will show you how to craft over 130 different items that will help you in every area of your game.

The Minecraft Book

Imagine Publishing Ltd
Richmond House
33 Richmond Hill
Bournemouth
Dorset BH2 6EZ
☎ +44 (0) 1202 586200
Website: www.imagine-publishing.co.uk

Head of Publishing
Aaron Asadi

Head of Design
Ross Andrews

Edited by
Adam Barnes & Jon White

Senior Art Editor
Greg Whitaker

Design
Perry Wardell-Wicks

Printed by
William Gibbons, 26 Planetary Road, Willenhall, West Midlands, WV13 3XT

Distributed in the UK & Eire by
Imagine Publishing Ltd, www.imagineshop.co.uk. Tel 01202 586200

Distributed in Australia by
Gordon & Gotch, Equinox Centre, 18 Rodborough Road, Frenchs Forest,
NSW 2086. Tel + 61 2 9972 8800

Distributed in the Rest of the World by
Marketforce, Blue Fin Building, 110 Southwark Street, London, SE1 0SU

ISBN 978-1909758063

IMAGINE
PUBLISHING

Contents

Features

Getting started

"The beauty of Minecraft is that you can play the game however you want, everything's in your hands"

Minecraft essentials

Advanced Minecraft

Glossary

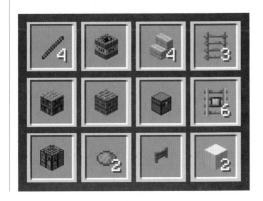

A guide to Minecraft

You may be familiar with Minecraft, but what do you actually do in it? We take a look at everything this world has to offer

Minecraft is a sandbox game in which you construct, create and develop worlds by manipulating blocks and items to make objects and buildings. It began life as an indie game in 2009, but it has grown into a multi-platform game with millions of players around the globe. Minecraft has become one of the most popular games in the world, thanks to its simple concept, originality and open

design. You are able to dismantle or add to the environment as you please. So, for example, you can build yourself a house or dig down into the ground. The entire world is destructible, and you can also use many items in the game to create new ones.

When you begin a game in Minecraft, a randomly generated world is created. Within this world are different environments known as biomes, which range from forests to snowy plains to huge oceans.

The worlds are massive, and it's highly unlikely you'll ever explore the entirety of one. Within each world, the game spawns specific areas like dungeons and villages that you might discover while playing.

There are two primary game modes in Minecraft. The first, and the one that is regarded as the true Minecraft experience, is Survival. In this you spawn in a world and must fend for yourself as the day switches to night. During the day the

world is largely peaceful, leaving you free to collect resources, build a home and hunt animals. At night, however, a host of hostile enemies known as mobs spawn, and you must defend yourself against them. If you die in this mode you respawn back at the point at which you first spawned, unless you sleep in a bed – your new spawn point. Dying will see

you lose any experience you have gained (although some of this can be retrieved) and you'll also drop all the items you were carrying, which you can also pick up again if you find the place that you died.

The other main mode of play in Minecraft is called Creative. In this, you are given access to all the items and mobs in the game and you can dictate

the sort of world you will spawn in. You cannot die in this mode, unless you fall off the bottom of the world, so it is a popular mode for users to create structures free from the restrictions of the day/night cycle of Survival mode.

As we've mentioned, though, however you choose to play Minecraft is up to you. While Creative is a fun mode, it is Survival that you will likely spend most time in and therefore this is the mode we've focused on in this bookazine. Minecraft is a huge game and it's unlikely you'll ever do everything, but we'll ensure that whatever you choose to do, this book will help you every step of the way.

"Minecraft has become one of the most popular games in the world, thanks to its simple concept, originality and open design"

Installing Minecraft

Learn how to download Minecraft and get yourself started in the game

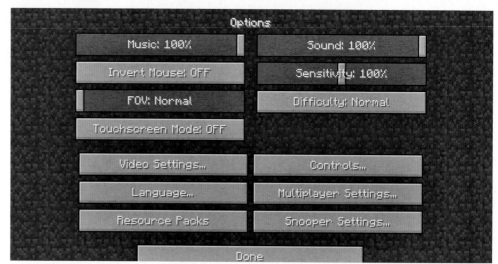

Fig 1: You can change your settings from the main menu in Minecraft

Minecraft is available on a number of different platforms. Throughout this bookazine we've focused largely on the PC version, but it's also available on Xbox 360 (and eventually the next-generation Xbox One), Mac, smartphones and Raspberry Pi.

On the PC, the system requirements are fairly minimal. You'll need an Intel P4 processor or equivalent, 2GB of RAM and the latest version of Java. For a full list of requirements, head to **help.mojang.com**. The game itself is tiny, just a few hundred kilobytes, although as you play it more and more and it renders new areas, this will grow – though only to a few megabytes.

To install the game on PC, make your way over to **minecraft.net** and, once there, you'll need to register a new account. This requires some simple details from you such as your email address, but it takes just a few minutes to complete. After you've done this you'll need to buy the game, which is £17.95, and then you can download it. Downloading the game is quick and easy, and it'll give you the launcher client that enables you to start the game.

On other platforms, you simply need to download the relevant app or game and it will be automatically installed onto your system.

Fig 2: Click on 'Singleplayer' to create a new world and get started

Fig 3: Add some multiplayer servers to play with other people online

Installing Minecraft on PC & Mac

Go to the site

The first step is to go to **minecraft.net** to get the game. Aside from being able to install the game here, this is where you'll find a lot of other helpful information. Click on the 'Buy Now!' button on the right-hand side to continue.

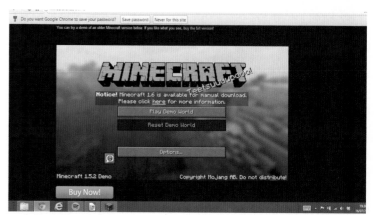

Play the demo

Before buying Minecraft we'd suggest that you try the demo, which is available below the 'Buy Now!' button. By playing the demo you can get a feel game and see if it's your cup of tea, and also see if your computer can run it adequately.

Register for Minecraft

After clicking 'Buy Now!' you'll be given the choice of buying the game for yourself or as a gift. Pick the former and you'll be taken through to a registration screen, where you'll have to enter just a few simple details.

Log in online

On the next page you'll be asked to verify your email address, once you've done this you'll be taken to your account. Now head back to the 'Store' at **minecraft.net** and, if you're logged in, you'll now be able to buy Minecraft.

Purchase Minecraft

On this screen you'll see the system requirements for the game, and below you'll be able to buy your game. Insert your payment details and you'll be sent a redemption link that will enable you to download the launcher.

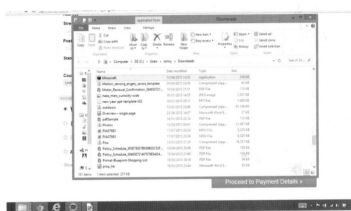

Find your download

When you're downloading the game, you'll want to check where you've downloaded it to. Check your Downloads folder or you might have a downloading toolbar that shows you your downloads.

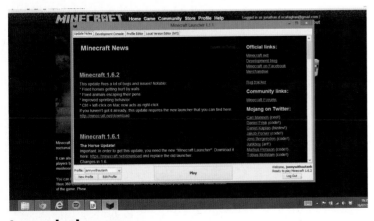

Launch the game

At this point you will have downloaded the **minecraft.exe** executable file. Clicking this file will bring up the launcher. Here you'll need to enter the details you registered with earlier before continuing to start the game.

Play the game

Congratulations! You've now installed Minecraft. At this point you'll be at the game's main screen. From here you can choose to start a game in Singleplayer or Multiplayer or check out some of the game's settings.

Controls

Find out how to control your character in the different versions of Minecraft

PC controls

The controls in Minecraft are simple, and they can be reconfigured if needed. The mouse is used to turn your player and move the camera in third-person mode. The mouse wheel scrolls through your inventory hot bar. Left-clicking is the default attack or dig button, while right-clicking uses the item currently in your hand. Clicking the mouse wheel will switch to the block being looked at in your inventory if it is available.

W, A, S and D keys move you forward, backward, left and right respectively. The space bar is used to jump, and can be double-tapped in Creative mode to fly. Left Shift puts you in sneak mode, and while held you won't fall off ledges. E brings up the inventory, Q drops the item you are currently holding and T brings up the chat window. The / key brings up the command window, while Tab shows a list of players if you are in a multiplayer game.

F1 toggles the Heads-Up Display on and off, while F2 will take a screenshot of your current view. F3 brings up a list of debug information including your current location and F5 toggles between first-person and third-person views.

Pressing F3 brings up the debug info in the PC version

Minecraft on Xbox 360 is very similar to its PC counterpart

Xbox 360 controls

The controls on Xbox 360 offer a similar level of functionality as on the PC. The right analogue stick is used to look around, and clicking it in will toggle your view between first- and third-person. The left analogue stick is used to move around, and will put you in sneak mode when clicking in. The A button is used to jump, while the Y button brings up the inventory. The X button opens your crafting menu, while the B button drops an item from the hot bar. To mine in this version you can hold the right trigger, while pressing it once can also be used to attack. Left trigger places blocks but also fires your bow, blocks with your sword and uses special blocks. The right bumper cycles right in the quick-bar, while the left bumper cycles to the left.

When crafting, the controls change to make it a bit easier on a console. The analogue sticks and the D-pad move the pointer, while the A button creates the item you have selected. The Y button quickly moves items, while the X button splits half of the selected stack of items. The right and left bumpers move you to different groups of items, while the B button exits the crafting table menu.

Mobile

If you want to free yourself of the constraints of your desktop monitor or TV, then why not give Minecraft a go on your smartphone or tablet. Available on a range of platforms, this slimmed down version of the game is a great way to create and explore, wherever you are. The touch-screen controls make everything extremely easy to use; swipe left or right to turn, use the on-screen D-pad to move forward, back, left or right, and tap the central button to jump. You can tap on an item to select it, or access more by tapping on the three-dotted icon.

Although the world isn't as vast as on desktop or console – and some elements aren't on offer – this is a great way to enjoy Minecraft, and you'll find yourself deeply immersed in no time at all!

What you'll be doing...

Different tools are good for different purposes in Minecraft

Building and destroying

Once you've got yourself settled in Minecraft, you'll no doubt want to start building things. At first it might just be a small abode, but later you'll learn to make minecart tracks, redstone circuits and much more. Minecraft allows you to build almost anything you can imagine. If you look online you'll see some of the amazing constructions people have made, from entire cities to recreations of science-fiction spaceships. On the other hand, in Minecraft the entire world is destructible. So anything you build you can also destroy. You can make TNT, which will enable you to blow up sections of the world, or you can simply mine your way into the ground or a mountain and take it apart. You can build or destroy anything you please.

Creating

Another main feature of Minecraft is creating items. In the game there are a number of resources that you can mine, and you can use these to create weapons, tools and other objects. This includes everything from maps to swords to buckets. At the back of this bookazine we've included a reference guide that shows you many of the things you can create.

To create items in Minecraft you'll be using the trafting table, one of the most useful things in the game. Here you can combine items to create new ones. For example, iron ingots placed in a 'V' shape will create a bucket. Many of the items you can create replicate their actual appearance; a bed, for example, is three pieces of wool placed atop three pieces of wood planks.

You can build new items by using a crafting table

You'll find a host of useful resources and other things underneath the Overworld

Mining

Mining in Minecraft is essential if you want to create items. Whether you're scavenging drops from enemies or digging underground, the more resources you find, the more things you'll be able to build. The worlds in Minecraft are created in layers (one layer is one block), starting at unbreakable bedrock at layer 0 to the very top of the game-world 255 layers high. Different items spawn at different layers underground, so you'll have to explore the depths of the world if you want to find what you're looking for. Underground you'll find caverns that contain different resources, while there are also dungeons that contain certain rare resources. To create and build items and structures, you'll need to mine to collect useful resources.

Surviving and exploring

The Survival mode is all about, well, surviving. You'll need weapons and armour to battle hostile enemies, so in turn you'll want to mine useful resources to create new useful battle items. Aside from fighting mobs, you'll need to eat to survive. You have a health bar that diminishes over time, and if it reaches zero you'll start losing. By hunting animals you can scavenge for food, or you can grow wheat and other crops to make your own food.

While you learn to survive you'll also explore the world around you. You'll encounter different biomes, find new areas underground and encounter friendly and hostile mobs alike. When exploring, survival is of the essence to ensure you don't lose experience and items.

Kill animals to get their meat and survive in the world of Minecraft

Understand the interface

⬚ Enemies
When night comes, enemies will spawn in the Overworld. Some will catch fire in daylight. When you're underground, mobs can spawn at any time.

⬚ Experience bar
The experience bar shows you how close you are to reaching the next experience level. You can gain experience by mining and fighting mobs.

⬚ Crosshair
In the centre of the screen is the crosshair, which is the central point upon which your actions such as mining or hitting will happen.

⬚ Animals
Animals in Minecraft can be killed for food and to gain items. You'll come across herds of specific animals in different areas.

⬚ Enchanting
To enchant items using an enchantment table in the game, you will need to trade in a suitable number of experience points.

⬚ Health bar
Taking damage from explosions, mobs, falling or whatever will decrease the health bar. It increases when you have a full hunger bar.

⬚ Hot bar
At the bottom is the hot bar from your inventory. You can scroll through this with your mouse wheel or use the numbers on your keyboard to select items on the bar.

⬚ Armour bar
By wearing armour you can have an added layer of protection. This will deflect attacks from enemies, although you'll still die if your health reaches zero.

⬚ Remove the HUD
If you want to remove everything in the Heads-Up Display for whatever reason, press the F1 key and you will simply see the view in front of you.

⬚ Hunger bar
When this bar is full you will regenerate health, but if depleted to zero you will begin to lose health, so make sure you stay well fed.

⬡ Chat
In multiplayer, pressing T will bring up the chat window, where you can talk to other players and see information from the server you are in.

⬡ Debug screen
Pressing F3 will bring up the debug screen in the top left. This contains information about your game, and also shows your co-ordinates so you can locate your position.

⬡ Time of day
The position of the Sun in the sky determines the time of day. Mobs will spawn when the Sun sets at night-time.

⬡ Inventory
Pressing E will bring up your inventory in the middle of the screen, where you can craft basic items, equip armour and access your items.

⬡ Oxygen bar
When you go under water, an oxygen bar will appear above your food bar. If this is depleted, you will begin to lose health until you get some air.

⬡ Environment
You can explore anywhere in Minecraft. Anything you can see you can walk towards. You are free to wander and explore the world as you please.

⬡ Plant life
Minecraft is populated by plant life. Flowers can be picked up and used for food or potions, so you might want to collect some of them.

⬡ Experience level
This shows you what level you are currently at in the game. You start at zero when you spawn and can work your way up by picking up experience points.

⬡ Jump bar
When riding a horse, a jump bar will appear at the bottom showing you how far and high you will jump whenever you press the jump button.

⬡ Render distance
You can set the render distance in the settings. A further render distance will let you see more, but the game may run slower on your PC.

The aim of the game

Now that you're ready to play, is there actually any real objective to Minecraft?

Strictly speaking, there is not true purpose to the Survival game mode of Minecraft. There are no missions, no side quests and no jobs for you to complete. The game is entirely open-ended and you are free to do what you want. While the game spawns many specific game-created areas like dungeons, you are not required to explore and find all of these. You are free to decide where you go, when you want, doing what you please.

That being said, there are some features of Minecraft that work you towards an eventual 'end' to the game. First of all, you start the game spawned in the Overworld (Fig 1). Here you must find items and create tools to survive your first night and ultimately thrive in the game (Fig 2). Once you're settled in the Overworld, you'll need to start mining in order to collect useful resources if you want to progress at all in the game (Fig 3).

Underground you will find a host of resources and items that will enhance your gameplay experience. Things like iron, gold and diamond will enable you to make stronger and better tools and armour, while these and other resources can be used to make entirely new resources. Mining underground is essential to really do anything in Minecraft. While mining, you will likely eventually come across some obsidian blocks which, when mined, will enable you to go into The Nether by building a Nether Portal (Fig 4). This is another area of the game with new enemies and blocks, and also Nether Fortresses that house enemies known as Blazes. The Nether is a dangerous place, but it is fun to explore; also, movement in The Nether moves you much further in the corresponding Overworld, so you can strategically place Nether Portals to cover large distances in the Overworld.

Last but not least, using an eye of Ender will enable you to find a Stronghold (Fig 5), and here you will find a portal that will take you to The End, another dimension of Minecraft full of Endermen, although there's not much else here. However, it is in The End that you can fight the Ender Dragon

and, if it's defeated, you will be given a story and credits before being transported to your spawn location. Although this is technically the 'end' of the game, you are still able to continue the game as normal once you have finished this section.

Ultimately, though, it is up to you to have your own adventure. While elements are included to give you a few goals to work towards, you are allowed to do anything you want in Minecraft with no limitations. Build a house in the sky, construct a roller coaster and so on. Whatever you choose to do, you'll have a great time discovering some of the originality that Minecraft has to offer. This sandbox game is like no other, and you'll spend hours on end doing completely different things every time you pick up the game.

Fig 1: You spawn in the Overworld, and it is here that your game begins as you explore and fight enemies

Fig 2: To survive and thrive in the game, you'll need to build your own tools, weapons and other objects

Fig 3: Once you've got to grips with the Overworld, you'll want to head underground to start mining resources

Fig 4: The Nether is a dangerous place, but you will no doubt want to explore it at some stage

Fig 5: Finding a Stronghold or constructing an End Portal will enable to go to the 'end' of the game, a dimension known as The End

"While elements are included to give you a few goals to work towards, you are allowed to do anything you want in Minecraft"

The different worlds…

The Overworld is full of animals, plant life and much more for you to explore

Survive the Overworld

There is a huge Overworld in Minecraft just waiting for you to explore. On the PC this realm generates itself infinitely into the distance, so you can never explore the whole thing (although, technically if you go 30 million blocks sideways the game will let you go no further). The Overworld is where you'll find the game's major components. Sections of the Overworld spawn in what are known as 'Chunks', areas of the game world 16x16x256 that spawn with different resources in them, although similar 'Chunks' spawn near one another. It is in the Overworld that you'll find all the friends and foes in Minecraft, as well as different biomes such as forests and frozen lakes.

Explore underground

Once you've mastered the Overworld you'll no doubt want to venture underground. Here, the same rules as above don't apply. Mobs can spawn in the darkness at any time of day, so make sure you bring torches with you. However, venturing underground is an essential part of Minecraft. Here you'll find all the resources you need to make new items in the game such as iron and redstone. Underground you'll also find some generated structures in the game. These include caverns, tunnels and caves for you to explore and find resources, although be warned that they may be full of enemies. Underground you'll also find dungeons with mob-spawning cages and other things, including abandoned mineshafts full of poisonous spiders.

Underneath the Overworld you'll find a multitude of useful resources

The Nether is a fiery, hellish dimension of Minecraft

Reach The Nether

The Nether dimension in Minecraft is one of the most dangerous places you can go. This fiery, hellish dimension is full of new enemies you won't find in the Overworld, like Zombie Pigmen and Blazes, while huge seas of deadly lava will kill you almost instantly if you fall into them. Ghasts, meanwhile, will launch firebombs at you that can set the world around you alight. Yes, The Nether can be a dangerous place.

Once you've accessed The Nether by building a Nether Portal, you'll find a number of useful items you won't elsewhere, so it is worth venturing there eventually. In The Nether you'll also find Nether Fortresses, where enemies known as Blazes spawn that can be killed for their useful blaze rod item drops.

Defeat the Ender Dragon

Some people regard the dimension known as The End as the technical end of the game. Of course, upon completing this section you are free to continue playing, but it can be a nice goal to work towards as getting many of the items necessary to reach The End can be a long and arduous process that feels like a mission of sorts.

Finding a Stronghold or constructing your own End Portal will bring you to this small world made of End Stone, and full of Obsidian Pillars and Endermen. It also plays host to the Ender Dragon, regarded as the final boss in Minecraft. Later in this bookazine we'll show you how to defeat the Ender Dragon, but you should know that it is not easy.

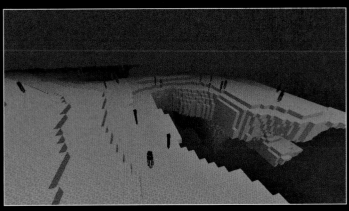

The End is populated by Endermen and the Ender Dragon

9 steps to surviving your first day

You've just spawned in a randomly generated Minecraft world, but what next? We'll talk you through the necessary steps to help ensure you make it through your first 24 hours in the Survival game mode

Of the three main game modes in Minecraft (Survival, Creative and Adventure), the Survival mode is the one that is branded as the 'true' Minecraft experience. The other modes are useful for messing around and creating maps, but for the proper single-player Minecraft experience it is Survival you should turn towards.

On your first play we would suggest sticking with the default settings for Survival; but after you've got to grips with it, feel free to utilise some of the settings to create new and varied worlds with specific things in them. For now, we'll start with the basics. To get started, go into the 'singleplayer' mode and click Create New World, give it a name, and then click Play This World after you've selected your created world

How you choose to play Minecraft is entirely up to you. Your randomly generated world is an open

canvas and there is no set way to play the game. There is also, strictly speaking, no way to definitively 'beat' the game, although confronting the Ender Dragon in The End is considered by some to be a sort of final boss battle.

Minecraft has a number of different biomes, which are areas with varying geographical features ranging from forests to oceans. You'll spawn in a random biome and from here on in it's up to you to create, build and survive your way through the game. A day in Minecraft lasts 20 minutes, with

day and night each lasting about ten minutes. This means that from the moment you spawn, you'll have about ten minutes before night falls.

At night a whole host of hostile mobs, which are enemy non-playable characters, will spawn, many of which will try to kill you. If you die you will lose all the items in your inventory and be sent back to your initial spawn point. To progress in Minecraft and build up your character's experience level you need to survive, so in this section we will walk you through your first day.

> "How you choose to play Minecraft is entirely up to you. Your randomly generated world is a completely open canvas and there is no right or wrong way to play the game"

1. Find some wood

So, you've just spawned for the first time in Minecraft. Now the real fun begins. The first thing you'll want to do is immediately take note of where you've spawned. This is where you'll respawn if you die, so don't stray too far from this spawn point until you've made a bed (more on this later) so you can find your way back to wherever you were if you die. You can also press F3 and note down your x, y and z co-ordinates if you want.

Now, the first thing you'll want to do is collect some wood. Wood is absolutely essential in Minecraft for building tools and objects. You've only got bare hands for now, but this is fine. Go up to a tree and hold the left mouse button on the trunk and you will begin mining. The wood block will break down and eventually be destroyed, leaving a floating miniature wooden block behind. Pick this up and then do this six more times to get enough wood to make tools and other things in the next steps.

2. Make a crafting table

Next we'll begin making some useful things. Press E to bring up your inventory. This is where you can order things to appear in your primary 1-9 slots at the bottom, which can be selected with the mouse wheel or with the numbers on your keyboard, and also store things in your general inventory in the middle. This is also where you can equip yourself with armour in the top left, which we'll talk about later in this bookazine.

The bit that we're interested in at the moment is the 2x2 crafting window in the top right. Place all the wood you have collected into one slot and it'll appear after the arrow as wood planks. Each block of wood will produce four wood planks. Click on the wood planks to pick up one batch and move them to your inventory, or Shift-click to convert all of the wood into wood planks instantly. Next, place one wood plank in each of the four crafting slots to make a crafting table (pictured), also known as a workbench.

3. Make a pickaxe

Your crafting table is what you'll use to make all your tools, weapons and other objects later in Minecraft. Place it in your inventory hot bar (the bar with nine slots at the bottom of your inventory) and press E to exit the inventory. Now select the crafting table using the mouse wheel or the corresponding number on your keyboard and place it on the ground. Right-clicking it will use it and bring up the expanded crafting options the crafting table offers.

In the crafting table, place one block of wood planks above another. This will create four sticks, which can be used to make tools. Take the sticks into your inventory and then place one in the middle square of the crafting table and another in the bottom middle. Along the top row, place three wood planks. This will create a pickaxe, which you can now put into your inventory. Pickaxes are used to speed up the mining process as they are much more efficient than your bare hands.

4. Build a shelter

By now you're probably almost halfway through the day, so night isn't far off. The best thing to do next is to build a small 3x2 shelter to protect yourself from the hostile mobs that will spawn when darkness falls. Use your newly acquired pickaxe to break your crafting table and pick it up, then find a suitable area in the side of a mountain or cliff and dig yourself a small shelter. Dig far enough in (or down) to find some cobblestone, which is a grey block noticeably different from brown dirt.

Place your crafting table down and put six wood planks in a 2x3 rectangle. This will make a wooden door. Use some of the dirt blocks you mined earlier to close up the entrance to your shelter so that there is only a one-block gap, and place the door here. Right-clicking the door will open and close it. Although not indestructible, wooden doors are useful for protection, and later you can make unbreakable iron doors by using iron ingots in place of wood planks.

5. Add some light

The next step is to make torches to add light to your shelter. Hostile mobs only spawn in dark areas, so torches are useful to keep you safe. A torch is made by placing a piece of coal or charcoal on top of a stick in the crafting table. Coal can be mined by finding cobblestone with black speckles on it. If you haven't found any coal yet, however, you'll need to make some charcoal.

To make charcoal, first use your pickaxe to mine some more of that cobblestone you found earlier. Once you've got eight blocks in total, head over to the crafting table and place all your cobblestone in a circle around a blank square in the middle of the 3x3 crafting grid. This makes a furnace, which you can then put into your inventory. Place the furnace down and right-click on it. Place wood planks in the bottom-left slot, and regular wood in the top slot. When it has finished burning, it will create charcoal, which you can use to make torches to light up your den.

6. Make a chest

Although you probably won't have a need for one quite yet, a chest is very useful to build. Chests can be used to store items rather than keeping them in your personal inventory, so when you go mining you've got more free space to pick stuff up. You can also place two chests next to each other to make a larger chest with double the space (54 storage slots compared to 27 for a small chest).

To make a chest, place eight wood planks in a square in the crafting table, like you did with the cobblestone to make a furnace. This will produce a chest that you can then put in your inventory. Select it and place it somewhere in your den. You'll want to eventually store any valuable items in your chests so that if you die, you won't lose any items you wanted to keep. Instead, they'll be kept safely in your den.

For an added tip, you can Shift-click to quickly transfer things back and forth between your inventory and the chest.

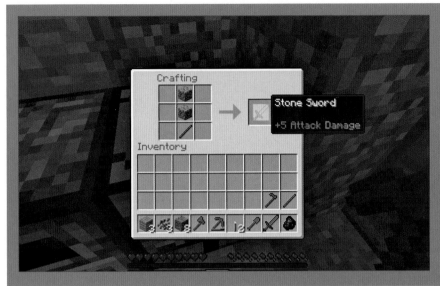

7. Craft other tools

Now it's time to make some other weapons and tools that you'll find useful. Hopefully you've still got quite a few wood planks and cobblestone; if not, quickly go and mine some more before it gets dark and then come back to your den.

Cobblestone can be used to make stone tools, which are comparatively stronger than wooden ones. Convert some wood planks into sticks in the crafting table. Using a combination of sticks and cobblestone, you can now make tools that are good for different purposes. One stick in the bottom-middle craft slot with two cobblestone blocks above it will make a stone sword, useful for attacking mobs. Two sticks below one block of cobblestone will make a shovel, which is the best tool for breaking dirt blocks. To make an axe for chopping wood, place one cobblestone above two sticks, then one cobblestone to the right of the first cobblestone and another below this next one. These are the most essential tools for now, but there are others you can make later on.

8. Make a bed

It is imperative that you build a bed, since the last place you sleep in Minecraft acts as your respawn point. This means that if you die, you'll spawn back at your bed; you can also sleep through the night when hostile mobs are on the loose.

Making a bed isn't easy. You need to find some sheep and collect wool from them. For now, you'll do this by killing them, but later you can learn to make shears that enable you to take wool from sheep without killing them. Sheep can be found in most areas, often grazing either out in the open or on cliffs. If you've already found some sheep, kill three to get three pieces of wool, then place the wool in a horizontal line above three wood planks on the crafting table to make a bed. If you haven't found sheep you'll need to go and hunt some down, but be sure to keep a track of where your home is in case you get lost.

9. Go to sleep

By now night will have fallen, so make sure you're in your den with your door closed. If any mobs have seen you then they might try to break down your door, so you'll have to kill them before you sleep. You'll want to expand your den at this point to make room for the bed, which takes up two blocks. As mentioned before, if you go to sleep your respawn point will be set at the last place you went to sleep.

Right-clicking on the bed will send you to sleep, although you can only sleep when it's dark and no hostile mobs are nearby. You will wake up the next day, when most hostile mobs left over from the night will catch fire and disappear. You're now ready to start your second day, free to do what you want. We'd suggest you either explore the world around your base, or begin digging down into the ground to find new useful items like iron. Do what you please; the world is yours!

Getting started

26

85

34

Minecraft: an overview

The awesomely creative game fully explained

While this section might seem like it's for beginners, there's so much depth to Minecraft that even if you've been playing for months, **you might find out something new.** Getting started is all about what to do in those first few weeks of the game, from surviving the night and dealing with monsters to recognising game worlds and settling down. It's vital to master the basics before you attempt anything like trying to explore caves and ravines. And if you're finding that despite your best efforts you're just dying over and over again, there might be something important that you've missed. Either way, having a strong base knowledge of not only the world itself but some of the mechanics behind it – how likely useful things are to spawn, where enemies come from etc – makes it a lot easier to succeed in the game.

This section acts as a guide for those just starting out, and a refresher course for seasoned adventurers. Covering game worlds, mining tips, farming, crafting and even the monsters you'll encounter, it's everything you'll need to make your way in the world of Minecraft. Whether you're looking to build expansive worlds or just have some fun, we've got it covered.

"It's vital to master the basics of the game"

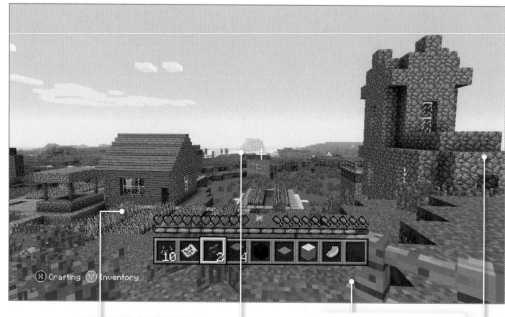

Crops
Growing and tending to your own crops can be a great way of creating resources

Villages
While this is a randomly spawning village, it's a good example of how your skills can eventually progress

Biomes
There are many different areas in Minecraft; here you can see in the distance a desert biome

Building
It might seem daunting to begin with, but soon you'll know how to create structures like this too

Staying alive
Get off on the right foot

We'll give you a lot more detail throughout this book, but getting started can be tough. First, you need to figure out what biome you're in. A biome is the area you're in; for example a jungle, or a snowy plain, or a cave. You should be able to look around and figure out which kind of biome it is; use our handy guide for tips on biomes and which ones are best for building shelters.

You'll need an immediate shelter, just in case you run out of time later on. Mine the ground for quick blocks to make a simple mud hut. Remember that a shelter needs to be fully enclosed to stop enemies. However, while it's good to get your shelter sorted, you won't have a bed yet (with a bed, you can choose to sleep through the night), so you'll probably want something to do at night time. In the day, mine as many resources as you can, particularly oak trees, and – if you can find it without going too far – coal to make torches. Coal does need a pickaxe, but you can make that easily with a crafting table made out of wood. When it gets dark, head back to your shelter, wall yourself in and spend the night crafting all kinds of useful things for the next day.

What you need to know

1: Exploring

From the time you first discover the map to that moment when it's all filled in, we guide you through exploring the rich worlds of Minecraft and what important and useful features to look out for.

2: Building

One of the key things is getting through your first night. If you can survive that, you're in good stead for creating a reliable base, building and expanding your home. We show you where is best to start.

3: Feeding

It's not as simple as 'kill animal, eat meat', unless you want to spend all your time hitting cows. From how to cook food properly to what you should avoid eating, we can save you a lot of trial and error.

4: Crafting

Starting off with fishing rods and buckets, crafting can eventually give you the skills to form portals to other dimensions, and create full diamond armour. There's always something new to learn.

5: Mining

From seeking out coal for torches and fuel, to surviving in the depths of fiery caverns, mining is a huge part of Minecraft. We'll show you where best to find what you're looking for, and how to mine it.

6: Farming

One of the more peaceful elements to Minecraft, the successful creation of a farm depends on a lot of hidden factors. Whether you want to improve your existing farm or get to know the basics, it's all here.

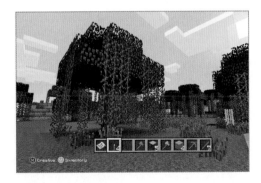

7: Game worlds

With so many different areas, it can be pretty tricky finding your way around. And there are so many things that only spawn in one place. With our guide, you'll never be lost for where to find materials again.

8: Creatures

Which ones are safe, which explode? Which make the tastiest meat, how can you farm them, where can they be found? There are a range of creatures in Minecraft, and not all of them particularly friendly.

9: Enemies

If this image doesn't strike dread into your heart yet, it soon will do. Read on for how to prevent various beasties from ruining your world, or even killing you. Pro tip: run away from these guys!

Understand the game worlds

A handy guide for adventurers, explorers and spelunkers

It's a pretty daunting experience, just being thrown into a world with little more than a map and the knowledge that when it gets dark, all manner of beasties are going to come crawling, jumping and exploding out of the depths of the world, so you'd better get building that shelter quickly out of whatever you can mine with your bare hands. Whether you're deciding where best to create a new dwelling – bear in mind you do need a bed to create a new respawn point wherever that bed is placed – or simply exploring the world for the first time, it's important to know what it is you're actually looking at, and how it can be useful to you. Some areas aren't great to start your home, others are easy to use, while a few can be adapted to be livable, depending on your skill level. There's so much creative freedom here that it's really worth familiarising yourself with what's available, and then once you know the basics, so many other things open up to you. Fancy a wolf pack for company? A cat to drive away creepers? Or are you trying to bake a cake and need to get hold of some of those elusive chocolate chips? Regardless, being aware of what each biome, or area, contains is one of the easiest ways to start getting really adventurous in Minecraft.

"There's so much creative freedom here"

River
Intersecting the two biomes, there are a lot of animals and plants around rivers

Forest
One of the most useful things to look for when starting: an oak forest

Sand
If you're not near a desert, sand near water can be used to make glass

Plains
With a river and forest within easy reach, this is the perfect place to set up a dwelling

Exploration

Finding the perfect spot for a shelter

The quickest way to find out more about the biomes is to enter Creative mode and take a flight around the landscape. From above, it's easy to see where each game world starts and ends, and the kinds of naturally occurring elements separating them, such as chasms and mountains. However, for the true adventuring experience, it's best to create yourself a shelter, then go exploring for anything interesting or useful. Some of the biomes, such as swamplands and plains bordering forests, are great to start a new shelter, so it's often worth having a scout around the area to see if you can find the best place. Other biomes, such as desert and snow plains, aren't ideal, though they can all be adapted to become places you can flourish in. Take care not to go falling down a chasm or go cave-exploring straight away. While these kinds of mistakes are arguably part of the learning curve of Minecraft, there's nothing more annoying than building up materials when scavenging only to run feet-first into a ravine and lose everything at the bottom. Be mindful when exploring the world and, for the first few days at least, keep it safe.

A guide to plains

The perfect biome for hunter/gatherers

These large, flat and lush areas are often home to lots of flora and fauna. Plains are home to most of the animals, including horses, which only spawn on plains. You will also often find NPC villages on the plains, which are a great place to find and trade resources. The plains are a great place to set up a home, if you can find an area close to some oak trees, as the flat terrain makes it easy to defend from enemies, as well as providing an easy landscape to shape into a farm or crop fields. Water is abundant in these areas, as are flowers and grasses, which can will often drop their seeds when mined. Plains are easy to identify by their light green grass and red earth, and are frequently bordered with a variety of trees. When exploring the plains it is much easier to find mines, caves and watering holes, though there are more enemies that roam the plains at night than some other areas.

The features of plains

1: Landscape
The plains are a good starting point to explore as you have a great field of vision. It's a little bland in terms of content, but still useful for more peaceful players.

2: Rain
You'll get caught in the rain sometimes. If out in the plains, you may as well make your way back to your house as the rain will really obscure your vision.

3: Water
Rivers and other water are often found on the borders of plains. Around the water you'll often find sugar cane and sand, making it a useful place to scavenge.

4: Extreme hills
Extreme hills are another kind of biome, often found connected with plains. It's a great place to mine as there can be caves, lava, trees and animals in these areas.

Explore deserts

Not as barren as it looks, there's a surprising amount to find here

While these biomes aren't the most provident of areas, there's still a lot to be found in the desert if you know what you're looking for and how to find it. Consisting predominantly of sand and a handful of plants, there are nonetheless advantages to exploring and mining in the desert. To start with, on account of the mostly flat terrain, it's easy to see enemies coming at you and hide/fight accordingly. Also, in the desert areas you can also find villages, wells and temples. Desert temples, also known as pyramids, can be identified by their ankh symbols, and contain traps and loot ranging from emeralds and diamonds to rotten flesh and bones. However, most deserts that you come across will seem pretty barren in comparison to the other areas.

The features of deserts

1: Cacti
Their spines can hurt you! You can mine these fireproof plants if you don't touch them; they can make a good barrier, but destroy any dropped items they touch.

2: Terrain
The desert areas are flat with the odd low-rising hill. Mine the top layer of sand for sandstone (use a pickaxe to harvest it) to make yourself a sand dwelling.

3: Sugar Cane
Sugar cane only grows next to water. Rare in the desert, it isn't impossible to find and is easy to spot. It can be crafted into both sugar and paper for crafting.

4: Survival
Animals don't spawn in the desert, so you're unlikely to find them there. Stock up on meat from animals in other biomes if you want to go exploring the desert.

Find your way through jungles

Lush and verdant areas, jungles are great for acquiring resources

There's just so much in these dense tropical biomes, from their tall jungle trees and vines to some elements only found in these locations, such as jungle temples. With most of the foliage a deep bright green and the biome itself often quite expansive, it can be a little confusing travelling around these areas, so be sure to create paths through the trees to help you keep your bearings.

Not only are there tall jungle trees to be found here, but also oak trees, making this a great biome to start off in. Treetop houses can also be built around the trunk of the tree, which can be a great way to defend yourself from various night-time

beasties. The jungle trees themselves are unique to the jungle biome and can sometimes grow into especially thick trees with four times the area of regular trees and usually considerably taller.

You can create a path through the canopy from a tree trunk, making it much easier to see where any enemies might be. However, to fully get the most from this biome, you will need to travel the area on foot, as the hilly, dense area can hide useful elements such as lakes and caves. You'll also find temples, ocelots and cocoa plants. Temples are large stone structures that often contain loot and traps – usually both – and are easily identified by

their mossy cobblestone appearance, as well as frequently being quite large.

The ocelots in this area are similar to wolves in that they are passive unless attacked, and they can be tamed. When tamed, with the offer of a raw fish, ocelots will change their skin colour and become cats, following you across the map if you befriend them – though unlike wolves, they won't actively attack your enemies. However, Creepers are afraid of ocelots/cats and will run away from them, so it's worth travelling into the jungle biome to find some – but bear in mind that ocelots will themselves run away from wolves even though they won't attack.

The hidden treasures of the jungle

1: Travel
The jungle biome is the densest of all the areas in terms of airspace. Create a path, light torches and mark your path in some way so that you won't get lost.

2: Ocelots
To tame an ocelot, you must be in an open space (7x7). Hold the raw fish and approach very slowly. It'll notice you and approach you, then you can feed it.

3: Temples
If you see cobblestone, it is likely there is a temple close by. Explore the area, but go into the temple well prepared, as there are often enemies and traps inside.

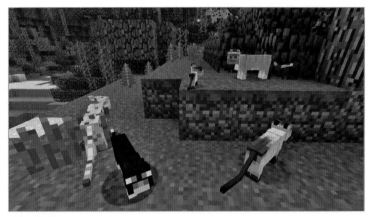

4: Cocoa pods
Only found in the jungle areas, cocoa pods can be mined for brown dye or to be used in the production of cookies. You can find them on jungle logs and trees.

Survive in the snow

This weather conditions can make life tough, but snowy biomes are plentiful

Snowy biomes are one of the most common in Minecraft. There are two main types: ice plains and taiga. Taiga landscapes are hilly and filled with dense, dark trees, while ice plains or tundra are large flat snowy areas. Both kinds of snowy area have a layer of snow covering the ground, and often contain wolves and frozen lakes and rivers that can be broken through.

While ice plains are some of the prettier areas in Minecraft, they are also one of the hardest to initially survive in, due to the lack of trees and wide expanse. Taiga biomes, though filled with trees, are hard to defend yourself in, since it's easy for monsters to sneak up on you. Here's what you can expect to find in these snowy landscapes.

Get to grips with snowy biomes

1: Taiga
Here you can see a little taiga biome. The trees are spruce, which aren't as good for getting started as oak since spruce cannot make a crafting table.

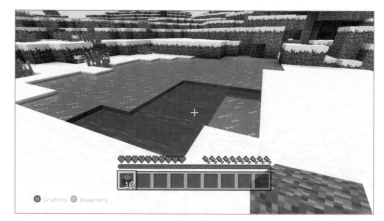

2: Ice
Ice can be broken to reach water. Use a shovel on snow to make snowballs, then craft them into blocks to create a shelter. Snow and ice melt near torches or lava.

3: Snow
Snowfall can be a major visual hazard, especially when it's getting dark. Ensure that you don't wander around too much, as it can also be very disorienting.

4: Exploration
There can be some very pretty surprises. Occasionally, flowers and sugar cane will spawn in these areas. It's always worth exploring to see what you can find.

The Nether

Fiery demons, lakes of lava, angry lost souls – welcome to hell

By far the hardest area to explore in Minecraft, this world is also home to some of the most useful materials, such as Netherrack and Glowstone. Only accessible via a Nether Portal, and surrounded by bedrock that cannot be mined, The Nether cannot be found on the original world map. However, distances moved in The Nether equate to eight times those in the Overworld, meaning that it can be used as a method for fast travel. Considerably dangerous to explore, The Nether is home to all manner of beasties, from fireball-shooting Ghasts, mobs of Zombie Pigmen, and fast-moving Wither Skeletons. All of these are very dangerous to encounter and should be fought with gold or diamond weapons, if you absolutely have to fight them.

The features of The Nether

1: Nether Portal
Build your Nether Portal, 4x5 blocks with corners optional, out of obsidian and light it with flint and steel or a fire charge. When activated, it will glow purple.

2: Lava
It's everywhere in The Nether, and deadly. It also sets a lot of materials on fire. If you want to travel across lava, you should bring some stone to make a path.

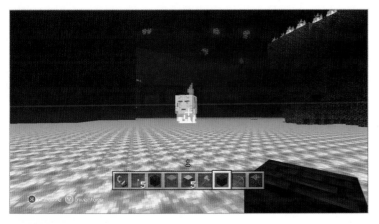

3: Ghast
There are a lot of dangerous enemies here, including these ghoulish creatures. They spit fireballs at anything in view, so use cover when travelling in The Nether.

4: Nether Fortresses
These are large bridges with rooms. Occasionally, you'll find chests of high-end loot like gold and diamonds, but more often Blazes and Wither Skeletons.

Traverse swampland

Look past the muddy exterior to find a range of useful items

These marshy, boggy areas are a mix of shallow water and darker grass with oak trees. A good starter area to explore, swamplands have a useful combination of wide and flat areas, with the addition of water making it easy to get away from surprise enemies. They're a good place to look for food, as animals are abundant, as well as sugar cane and mushrooms. Mushroom-hunting is particularly easy, as many clusters of them can be near watery areas and also inland.

The water parts of the swampland are very shallow, with a mix of sand, clay and dirt as the bed. The swamplands are a useful biome to go to if you want to pick up a lot of different materials all at once, and though it might not be the area you eventually settle in, it's easy to make a quick and durable shelter out of the materials that you can find in this biome.

The trees in this area are covered in green vines like the jungle, though it is easy to distinguish the swampland from the jungle as the trees are much sparser and don't grow nearly as high. There are also far fewer of them, and the colour palette is much less vibrant than the jungle. However, the vines themselves can be pretty useful, as you can use them for ladders while you are in sneak mode. You can then use them to climb up trees to get a better view of the area, and for your own dwelling in place of a ladder.

One of the rather more dangerous elements of the swampland is the Witch Hut. While the hut itself is filled with mushrooms and useful elements such as a crafting table and cauldron, every Witch Hut contains a Witch. These look like regular villagers, only with grey skin, purple robes and a black witch hat. Combat with a Witch can be risky, as they will throw various potions at you that affect your health and status, but when killed they can drop some very useful items, from glowstone dust and glass bottles to sticks and sugar.

What you'll find in swampland

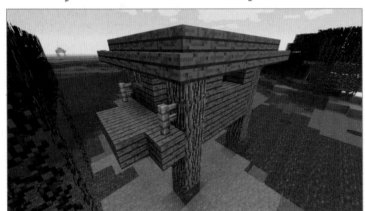

1: Witch Hut
While the Witch Hut is filled with goodies, be wary of the Witch. The hut itself is made out of spruce wood planks and can spawn on both watery and dry areas.

2: Shallow water
You can fish anywhere in water, as long as you have a fishing rod. As well as a quick source of food, fish are the only way to befriend an ocelot (in the jungle).

3: Mushrooms
There are lots of mushrooms in the swampland, which you can use to make soup. It's quite a rich biome in terms of nature, so good to stock up on food.

4: Lily pads
You will often see lily pads in swampland. These are useful to mine as they can be walked on without falling into the water, so you can build bridges easily.

Explore chasms

Take torches, a pickaxe and meat; let's go spelunking

Chasms, or ravines, are scars across the landscape: tall, long expanses of empty space in the world, surrounded by grey stone. When adventuring in the mountains, you must be especially careful as most drops into a chasm will kill you. These chasms can give way to caverns, abandoned mineshafts, caves, dungeons etc. Though they are dangerous, they are well worth exploring fully if you've got the right equipment.

The majority have their highest point/entrance on the surface, but chasms can be found at any level. It's well worth your time to load up on the essentials – a strong pickaxe, food for the journey – but bear in mind that you will be travelling a long way underground, so make sure to leave all of the valuables you have found or crafted so far at home and only take what you need, which should definitely include plenty of torches. Even if you want to just explore a little, you can often find coal around the opening of the chasm.

There isn't any good way to search for chasms, but they are usually obvious and often appear between two biomes. Occasionally, they will appear hidden from view as they intersect with a hill or mountain, but keep a sharp look out for the solid grey stone and you shouldn't have too many accidents.

Inside the chasms themselves, you can find any number of creatures, from Spiders and Slimes, to good old Zombies and Creepers. Slimes – a single green block that will hop towards you – aren't so common in the rest of the world. If you see one you should attack it, as it will break into lots of little Slimes, which you can then attack for Slimeballs – used for crafting. Because chasms are so deep, they will often expose a variety of ore, such as diamond or gold. Some chasms even go so deep as to expose the lava lakes nearly at the base of the world. So the further you go into a chasm, the more watchful you will need to be.

Discover what lies inside a chasm

1: Finding chasms
They're usually pretty easy to spot, but sometimes you'll just fall into one and it can be a real hassle getting all your equipment back from the bottom.

2: Exploring
This is the opening to a ravine between two hills. It's vital to be prepared before you go down, as chasms can incorporate most other underground structures.

3: Assessing
Take a look along the side of the chasm and there are usually access points. You may need to jump down a little, so ensure your food bar is full to regain health.

4: Into the dark
Chasms can contain useful things, like this pink iron ore. Sadly, they are also host to some exploding enemies, like this Creeper. Always keep a sharp lookout.

A look inside mineshafts

Hard to find and full of danger, but well worth exploring

Mineshafts are one of the trickiest areas to get to, aside from The Nether. You can find them by exploring chasms and caves, though they are relatively rare compared to other structures such as villages, and certainly more difficult to find. It will usually take a lot of exploring the underground areas before you find one, but it is worth looking for them – particularly in chasms, which can contain useful and/or precious ore regardless. Search the world for grey stone openings, and follow them carefully down as far as they will go. If a mineshaft is there, you will often find a large open room at the start of it, usually with several exits to choose from.

The corridors you will travel down are small, 'supported' by beams and wooden fences, and will frequently have old minecart rail tracks – and possibly minecarts. Often filled with great ore to mine, the mineshafts also contain chests of valuables. The hard part here is actually finding them, as most mines are like mazes, with lots of tunnels that intersect and branch out. Some will combine with other underground structures, like chasms, ravines and dungeons, but by far the most useful are those that open the area out and make spotting precious ore easier, particularly as any open sections usually contain a bridge of some kind.

The abandoned mines are usually teeming with enemies, so take care to light the way really well. Cave spiders are very common and also venomous, so watch out for them. There are also a lot of Creepers and Zombies in the mines, but the spiders are the ones you need to worry about, as their webs are also tricky to deal with. You can use your sword to cut them down, but if you don't want to wear your sword out, you can also use flint and steel to set fire to them. The most important thing when exploring the mineshafts is to be careful, as it's easy to get lost and hard to find your way again once that has happened.

Find out what mineshafts have to offer

1: Tunnels
The mineshaft tunnels usually contain tracks and wooden supports, so you can tell you've moved away from a regular cave and into an area worth exploring.

2: Chests
Containing anything from melon seeds and bread to diamonds and horse armour, the chests here can be some of the most fruitful in the game.

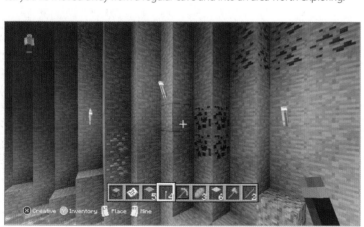

3: Ore
Some of the best ore can be found in mineshafts. This one has opened up into a chasm and left a lot more ore exposed than would normally be the case.

4: Navigating
It can be hard to keep your bearings in mineshafts, as so many of the corridors look the same. Find some way of keeping a note of where you've been.

Visit villages

Whether you're looking to rob and pillage or stay and help, villages can be very varied

Villages can be any size, from a well and a single building to several structures of a varied nature. While you can mine the buildings and their contents to take for your own – and this can be quite useful at the start of the game – it's much more rewarding in the long run to begin trading with the villagers and using what's there, such as crafting tables in libraries and lava at the blacksmiths. There are a lot of useful items to be found in villages, such as crops and animals, though villages do often come under attack at night from Zombies and other enemies. You can expand and even create villages yourself eventually; but to begin with, it's worth getting used to how a natural village operates.

The key features of villages

1: Finding villages
Villages are found only in the plains and desert They are relatively common, though, so keep an eye out along the skyline for any of the taller structures.

2: Desert village
While not as useful, desert villages have mostly the same structures as those on the plains. It's only the textures and materials that are different.

3: Villagers
Your popularity in a village can go up or down depending on how you treat the villagers. Hitting and killing them is obviously bad; trading with them good.

4: Hiding
There are several structures you can hide in at night, or you can fight the Zombies. Villages can be protected with befriended wolves and iron golems.

Mining overview

Ores, axes and lots of digging

Well, you had to guess this part was coming up. It is called Minecraft after all. Even during the early stages of any Minecraft world, you'll need to get quickly accustomed to digging, mining and ore-gathering, otherwise you're not going to get very far and those creeps are going to be banging at your door before you know it.

In this section, we're going to take you through exactly what you'll need and what you should be looking out for on your block-powered travels through the cubic underworld. While you might be comfortable with some basic crafting and excavating by now, chances are you haven't headed down into the depths and started mining for real. This is where the game really opens up and you start understanding the vast subterranean world Mojang has simulated for players brave enough to discover it.

So light up your torches, make a few fires, grab your pickaxe and let's get digging. There's some precious stuff under there, and this is how to get to it.

"You'll need to get quickly accustomed to digging, mining and ore-gathering"

Creepers
Just because you're happy mining, doesn't mean your enemies are. As always, you'll have to watch out for baddies

Track
It'll take skill and concentration, but building a track to get your ore to the surface is vital for advanced miners

Torches
Vital for lighting the way. Without torches, you're not going to be able to see a thing down there

The mine
It's called Minecraft, and this is why. Get digging underground and you can cave out your very own little space

Debugging it
Sometimes it pays to cheat… or at least get a bit more info

While you could just start your mine anywhere, it pays to do it in the optimum place on your map. In order to find this, you'll need to hit F3 and access the game's extensive and initially rather complicated debug menu. From here, you'll see a bunch of attributes all assigned to different letters.

You're going to want to move the Y attribute to 11, as that will be the best place to start mining – it'll be the level where every single ore is at its most abundant, and there won't be any pesky water or lava directly where you start to mine.

If you'd rather play more organically and scout out a good mining spot without the need to feel like Neo in *The Matrix*, then it's best to look for pools of lava, which tend to form around that mystical level 11. Alternatively, you could even dig down to bedrock, find the uppermost piece of bedrock, climb six blocks, and start there.

Or you could just ignore all of this and start digging where you want. Chances are your first proper mine isn't going to go as smoothly as you might like, so don't fret too much about its exact location. Just dig, experiment and enjoy.

Key features

1: Digging it up

You're not going to get very far without a decent pickaxe to get rid of all those pesky blocks in the way. Trying to start a mine with a basic axe is going to be a struggle, so make sure you start crafting better axes as soon as possible.

2: Watch out

You might be totally wrapped up in your diamond-hunting exploits, but those Creepers are not going to give two hoots about that. Make sure you've got a safe place to hide when it all goes wrong, and don't ever get too cocky.

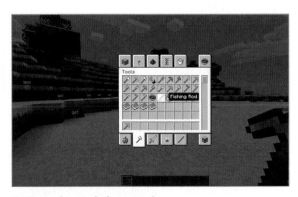

3: Supply and demand

The day you decide to venture into a giant mine without supplies is the day you realise that was a bad idea. We'll talk in depth about what you need to succeed in the underground, but whatever you do in Minecraft, make sure you're prepared.

4: Hot lava

There's not a great deal of use in building the world's greatest mineshaft if lava ends up pouring all over the place and burning your tracks and yourself. Be careful around those glowing orange pools and always, always bring a water bucket with you. It'll turn the hot liquid into obsidian, and you'll feel like a genius.

"Always, always bring a water bucket with you"

5: Snakes and ladders

Mines aren't safe for two reasons. One, they have monsters in them. Two, they're deep. If you want to get out of your mine, then you're going to need a ladder. It's also a good way of escaping if you get overwhelmed by bad guys. Don't be the miner who digs all the way to the bottom of the world and then realises he's got no way of getting back up. And yes, most of us have done that.

Mine types

There are more than two ways to mine in Minecraft

Just like in real life, there are plenty of ways in which you can actually mine in Minecraft. From basic cave-hunting to a full scale quarry operation, the room for experimentation and ideas is almost limitless.

To get started, it's probably best to scope out a few existing caves and see what's in there – that'll get you the basic resources you need to start actually mining. And you never know, with a few well-placed swings of a pickaxe or digs of a shovel, you might break through into a vast vault of goodness just waiting for you to nick it all. Or you might find a mob of nasties and end up getting the fright of your little square-headed life.

Once you're feeling confident, though, check out all these options for mine types, and see which one suits you. Don't get too ambitious, though, or you might just cave yourself in.

Learn the different types of mines

1: Spelunking
The funny word for general cave hunting and potholing. A great place to start, and if you get lucky, you might happen upon a bounty of riches.

2: Shaft mining
Vertical mining is a dangerous game, and requires plenty of preparation work and resources, but is one of the best ways to guarantee a good haul.

3: Horizontal mining
A bit easier, but you'll need patience. This involves digging down then across to make long tunnels. From there you can make branching tunnels.

4: Strip mining
Climb a mountain, blow up the top few layers with TNT, and start mining within. This is a lot easier than shaft mining, but requires a lot of explosives.

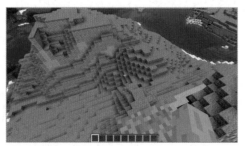

5: Quarry mining
Dig a giant pit with a staircase all the way down. To build an effective quarry, you should know where to mine in the first place. Check the debug menu.

6: Random mining
What most players do. Get a shovel and just start digging. It's inefficient, time-consuming and arduous, but so satisfying when you strike it lucky.

Mining tips

What to do when you're starting out your lucrative mining career

As with everything in Minecraft, you'll often spend as much time making progress as you do making mistakes. If you want to sidestep all that boring learning business, you're going to want to know the four most important tips for starting your mine properly.

Before you get to any of that, though, it's probably worth logging onto another Minecraft server and investigating someone else's mine so you can get a general feel for the place. There's so much work to do before you get to carving out precious stones that it's well worth doing your research. At least dive onto YouTube and scope out a few cavernous digging spots.

And now, if you're ready, here's where you're going to want to start. Happy hammering!

Top mining advice

1: Heat and eat
You should build plenty of fires in the halls of your mine, so you can cook food. Otherwise your time mining will be over before it starts.

2: Safehouse
A small room in the mine with its own furnace and a crafting table is essential, and it's somewhere you can escape to if things go wrong.

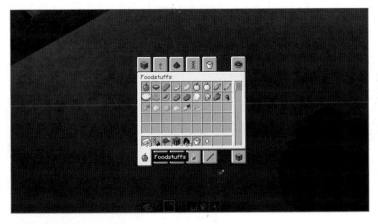

3: Food for thought
Make sure you are stocked up with provisions because it's very easy to get lost down there – and with no food, you're in trouble.

4: Torch light
Make sure you've got plenty of torches. You'll need to light the way along every corridor. No one wants to get lost in the dark with monsters about!

Transport material using minecarts

Once you've mined it, it's time to get all that goodness up to the surface!

Unless you're planning to build the next London Underground, you'll want to get all your precious materials up to the surface. And the best way to do this, unquestionably, is with minecarts.

Your choices will depend on resources. To craft the powered rails you'll need gold, redstone and the all-important stick. So as you mine for gold, you can build more rails, then get more gold…

To craft the carts themselves, you'll need a regular minecart and a furnace. At first, it makes sense to gather up some gold and make a short rail back to the surface, adding to it as you gain more resources. Make sure you've got enough track to support your onward journey into the mine, else you'll be making a lot of boring (and potentially dangerous) trips back and forth.

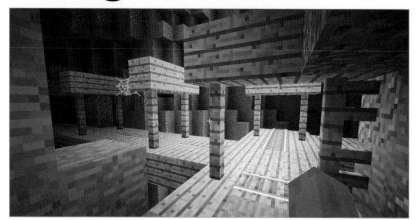

A guide to using minecarts

1: Cart life
You'll need minecarts. Get yourself to a crafting table, get your iron ingots out and make a cart. Craft that with a chest and you've got a storage cart. Perfect.

2: Rail talk
With gold, redstone and stick, you can make powered rails to automatically send carts to the surface. Place the tracks wisely and you'll soon be a mining tycoon.

3: Indiana clones
Carts aren't just for transporting your wares, either. Should you need to get somewhere quickly, you can dive into a standard cart and ride the rails yourself.

4: Multiplayer mining
A co-op partner can be working on the surface, waiting for your filled carts to arrive as you mine below. Take it in shifts and you can feel like a real miner.

Stay safe down the mines

It can get pretty hairy out there, so here are some top tips on how to stay safe

Without dropping the game down to Peaceful mode, Minecraft can be a dangerous place. You already know about Creepers and other such nasties wandering about at night-time, ruining all your hard work, but there are many other treacherous threats to worry about when you're digging deep and looking for the good life.

For starters, you could starve. More importantly, and less obviously, though, are cave-ins. Not only can they ruin you, they can ruin your mine. Imagine digging into a large water source when you've got your mine all ready, and the whole thing fills with the wet stuff and your entire plan is ruined. Now imagine how much worse that would be if it was lava. Check out these handy hints for staying safe underground…

Ways to keep safe while mining

1: Back the way you came
Go back the same way you entered the mine instead of trying to dig yourself a short cut. It could easily collapse and kill you or ruin all your hard work.

2: Don't take valuables
You do not want to lose all sorts of valuable materials when you're scouting out a new mining spot. Better to die with a stick than a pocket full of gold.

3: Bring a sword
It's not going to be safe down there, and you're going to need to defend yourself at some point. Make sure you're not the guy stuck without a weapon.

4: Water bucket
Make sure you have a water bucket handy. It's needed to put out fires and if you place yourself correctly, you can pour it on lava to turn it into obsidian.

Coal
Here's coal in the wild. Get pickaxing and get that good stuff out of there

It's mine
Whether you're caving or you've built your own mine, coal will be the most abundant mineral you find

Torch craft
Crafting torches – you're going to need to do this if you want to get anywhere underground in Minecraft

Silk Touch
Your pickaxe can get you small amounts of coal, but enchant it with Silk Touch and you can start mining the actual ore, which gives you much more coal

Learn to mine coal

The first thing worth mining, and the keystone to much of Minecraft's complexity

Coal is pretty abundant in Minecraft, being the only ore that appears both above and below sea level. As always, it runs in veins in-between stone blocks, and in this case you're going to need a pickaxe enchanted with Silk Touch in order to actually get the coal ore (an unenhanced pickaxe will just drop regular coal, meaning you're going to have to do a lot more legwork for your results).

Now, coal is going to be your best friend when you go hunting underground for more precious ores. It's required to craft torches (without which you're not going to be able to see anything underground), and you're also going to need it to fuel fires to cook food.

Of course, you can also do this with charcoal, which you can get by burning wood blocks, but that's neither as interesting nor as fulfilling as mining some good old-fashioned coal.

Finding coal and using it

1: Get a pickaxe
It's a pretty obvious starting point, but you're not going to get very far in a game called Minecraft if you don't have anything to mine with. Craft yourself a pickaxe as soon as humanly possible.

2: Enchant the pickaxe
Using an anvil or enchantment table, you can enchant your pickaxe with Silk Touch, which will allow you to gather previously unobtainable blocks like grass, cobwebs and, of course, coal.

3: Locate some coal
It's pretty easy to find: black dotted blocks are coal, just waiting for you to axe them up and collect their goodness inside. It's the only ore available overground too, so you don't even have to cave.

4: Make some torches
With coal in hand, you can now make torches, which are required for all mining duties. Get back up to the surface, craft as many torches as you can, and then you can keep mining.

5: Make a fire
With coal, you can fuel a fire. That fire can be used to cook food. Food can then be eaten so you can stay alive. And if you're not alive, you can't mine. It's a fairly simple equation.

6: Make a furnace
A furnace is also fuelled by coal, and can be used to smelt ores to get more useful items. It's a good idea to build a furnace in your home, and another in your mine. And always have enough coal to fuel it.

7: Get some charcoal
Just burn some wood blocks and you'll get charcoal. According to Notch himself, it's exactly the same as coal, it just has a different name. It goes to show how important this stuff is.

8: Power your minecarts
If you're really getting your mine going, you'll need a minecart. And they only work with coal or charcoal. Once you've crafted your carts, get those bad boys fuelled up with coal.

9: Kill a Wither Skeleton
Okay, so it's not the most efficient use of your time, but Wither Skeletons will occasionally drop a lump of coal when they're killed. And you'll also get that juicy XP for doing it, so get that sword out.

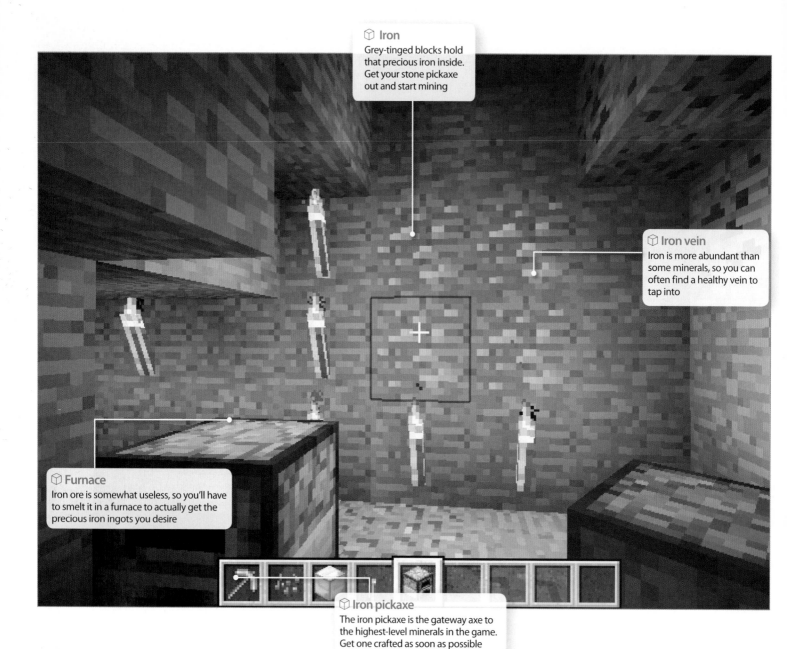

Iron
Grey-tinged blocks hold that precious iron inside. Get your stone pickaxe out and start mining

Iron vein
Iron is more abundant than some minerals, so you can often find a healthy vein to tap into

Furnace
Iron ore is somewhat useless, so you'll have to smelt it in a furnace to actually get the precious iron ingots you desire

Iron pickaxe
The iron pickaxe is the gateway axe to the highest-level minerals in the game. Get one crafted as soon as possible

Source iron

Tough, hard and metallic. A very important element in the world of Minecraft

Iron is a vital component in the Minecraft world. Not only is it useful for crafting mid-level tools, armour and equipment, it's also the stepping stone to mining the more powerful minerals, as you'll need an iron pickaxe to dig up diamonds.

In order to actually get the useful iron ingots, though, you'll need to build a furnace and smelt the raw iron ore down into a usable form. And what does this mean? It means that you will have to keep a steady supply of coal going as you mine for iron.

As long as you can maintain the balance of fuel and ambition, you'll be a strong iron miner in no time. And it's not just tools you can make – there are tons of clever uses for that iron that you may never have even thought of.

Find and use iron

1: Pickaxe time
You'll need a stone, iron or diamond pickaxe to mine for iron, so don't start hitting it with a stick as you won't get anywhere. Diamond is obviously best, but stone will do.

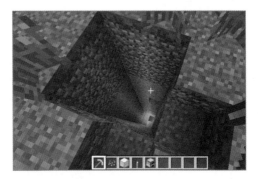

2: Delve deep
Iron is fairly abundant, but you won't find much of it above ground. The best thing to do is find a decent-sized cave and start looking for iron in there. If you do find some, it might be worth digging nearby.

3: Furnace time
Iron ore is pretty much useless on its own, so you're going to have to smelt it down in a furnace in order to make iron ingots. It might be worth building a second furnace in your mine for convenience.

4: Iron craft
Once you have a nice amount of iron, you should probably craft something with it. A great place to start is tools, so get that iron pickaxe if you don't already have one.

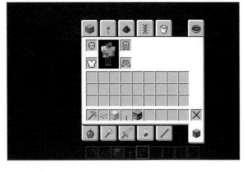

5: Suit up
Your next batch of iron should be used to make iron armour, so you can become the blocky Tony Stark you always dreamed of being. It'll make you tougher in fights, too.

6: Kick the bucket
You'll need iron to make a decent bucket, great for transporting water (which can then be poured onto lava). A worthy companion on any mining quest, as you'll find out the first time you fall in lava.

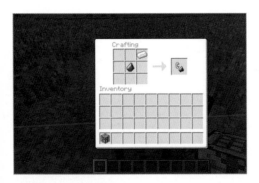

7: Flint and steel
You can use iron to craft flint and steel. If you're looking to make a fire – and you should be, as you'll need one to cook – then you're going to need flint and steel.

8: Compass
You'll be wanting a compass if you don't have a very good sense of direction. Crafting with iron and a bit of redstone will get you this useful item, which shows you your spawn point.

9: Traps!
Iron is often used to make traps which then damage other players in the Minecraft world. Always make sure you're aware that other players can lay traps for you near good mining spots.

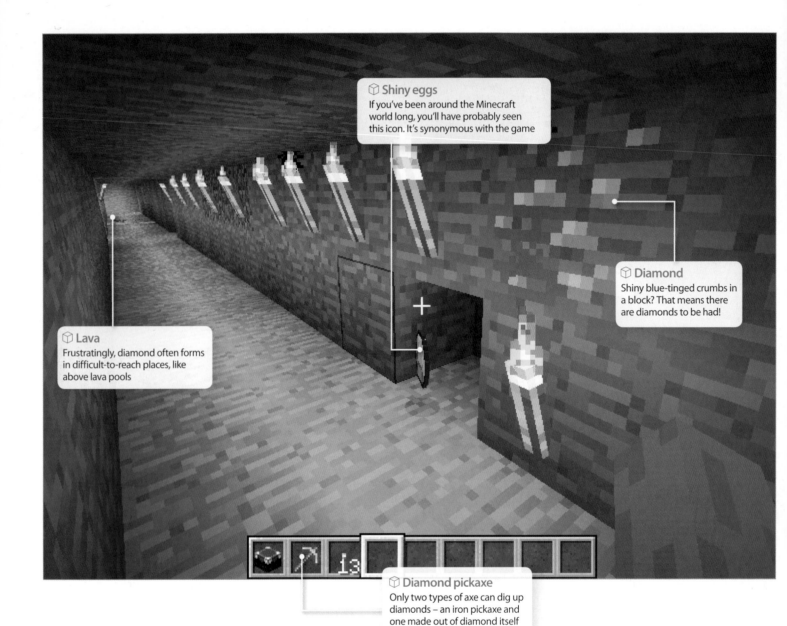

Shiny eggs
If you've been around the Minecraft world long, you'll have probably seen this icon. It's synonymous with the game

Diamond
Shiny blue-tinged crumbs in a block? That means there are diamonds to be had!

Lava
Frustratingly, diamond often forms in difficult-to-reach places, like above lava pools

Diamond pickaxe
Only two types of axe can dig up diamonds – an iron pickaxe and one made out of diamond itself

Dig for diamonds

It's very precious. You know you want it

Diamond is probably the gem most synonymous with all of Minecraft. Its blocky, pixellated icon can be seen on countless T-shirts at Minecon and on the profile pages of many a Facebook and Twitter account.

It's the most valuable mineral in the game, and therefore probably the hardest to mine. It can be used for all sorts of high-level items, such as swords, armour and the most powerful pickaxe in the game. And you can craft an Enchantment Table with it, meaning you can take your Minecraft game to the next level.

You're not going to be able to just start mining diamond straight away, though. It'll take preparation, the right tools, a hell of a lot of torches and just a touch of luck. So, before you get down into the depths and start looking for the shiny stuff, check out these must-read tips.

Find and use diamonds

1: Get the right pickaxe
A standard pickaxe won't cut it in the world of diamonds. You're going to need to craft an iron axe – or, if you've already got diamonds to hand, a diamond one.

2: Locate diamonds
Diamonds are usually found between the tenth and eleventh levels underground, so you'll need to find a deep cave or get digging yourself. Always keep an eye out for those blue/white-tinged blocks, though.

3: Hot lava
The deeper you go, the more dangerous it gets. Lava pours freely in the lower levels, and diamonds are often located near the orange stuff. Make sure you don't accidentally crate a lava spillage.

4: Craft a pickaxe
If you haven't already done it, get yourself a diamond pickaxe. It has more durability than anything else you can use, so you can keep mining for longer without having to switch out.

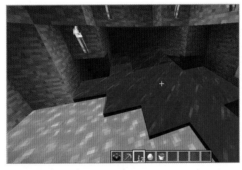

5: Mine some obsidian
If you've got a diamond pickaxe and you've poured water on lava, you can mine the obsidian it creates. There's no other way of getting obsidian, so while you're there you might as well grab it.

6: Craft an enchantment table
Once you have a supply of diamonds, it's a good idea to craft an enchantment table for your home. You'll need obsidian, diamonds and a book. The table can then be used to enchant other items.

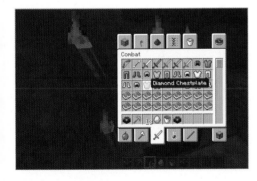

7: Craft diamond armour
If you want to survive mob attacks, you're going to need the toughest armour in the game. Get yourself some diamond armour and you'll feel almost invincible out there.

8: Craft a diamond sword
And if you are going out looking for a fight, you might as well get the most durable sword in the game, too. A diamond sword cuts through Creepers like a blocky knife through blocky butter.

9: Craft a jukebox
There are 12 songs in the game, and they can be played by building your very own jukebox. You'll need diamonds and a ton of wooden planks, and then a music CD. Enjoy the tunes!

Top tips

⬡ Redstone
Redstone appears as red-tinged blocks. It needs a stone pickaxe or higher to mine.

⬡ Machines
Connect redstone wire to a machine to power it. It's as simple as that.

⬡ Redstone wire
Placing redstone dust on the ground in a line turns it into a wire.

⬡ Redstone repeater
The power will only travel for 15 blocks, so you'll need a redstone repeater to create longer wires.

Search for redstone

Looking to get a little technical? Then look no further than redstone

It might not be the most valuable mineral in Minecraft, but it's hard to argue that redstone isn't the most useful. This vital ingredient can be found in sizeable veins underground, as well as a drop from certain enemy types.

Unlike the other minerals mentioned in this section, redstone has extensive uses beyond basic crafting. It can be used to power any of the game's machinery, simply by laying it on the ground like circuitry. This is how a novice Minecrafter can turn him or herself into an electrical wizard in just a few hours.

It's also a crucial ingredient in potion brewing, and can be used to change the base function of any concoction you might be trying to create. Ultimately, you're going to need a lot of redstone if you want to take your Minecraft world out of the dark ages and thrust it into modernism.

Finding and using redstone

1: Find redstone ore
Get down underground and hunt for red-tinged blocks. They typically run in pretty large veins, so it won't be too hard to gather a decent amount fairly quickly. You only need a stone pickaxe, too.

2: Kill a witch
Another excellent way to gather redstone is to kill a witch. More often than not they'll drop redstone. So if you're more of a fighter than a miner, you can get your electrical goodness that way.

3: Trade with priests
The third way to grab a good deal of redstone is to trade with village priests. They typically hold a great deal of redstone, and you can get a good price on the red stuff if you bring enough to sell.

4: Redstone torches
To get into the world of Minecraft circuitry, you'll need to craft some redstone torches. These act as power sources for all the machinery you want to run, as well as helping to light the environment.

5: Redstone wire
Laying redstone on the ground creates redstone wire, which acts as circuitry. Connect a redstone torch to a machine with wire to power it. It's very easy to lay the circuits, so start experimenting.

6: Redstone repeaters
To create a circuit over a long distance, you'll need to craft redstone repeaters. These allow a circuit to carry power over 15 blocks. They require redstone torches, stone blocks and redstone.

7: Powered rails
To get your minecarts moving, you'll need to create powered rails. Simply craft with six gold ingots, a stick and some redstone. Obviously, to make a long track, you're going to need a lot of gold!

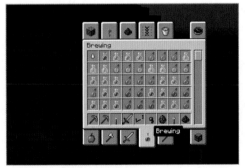

8: Brew some potions
Another fantastic use for redstone is in the brewing of potions. You can brew health-regenerating ones, fire-resistance potions and even drinks that help you see in the dark. Get brewing and see what you can find.

9: Play around
One of the best things about redstone is the world of possibility it lays before you. Try experimenting with machinery and wire to see what you can create. It might just blow your mind!

An overview of farming

Useful tips to get you started with farming

Farming in Minecraft will be your go-to method of obtaining sustainable food, both at the beginning of the game and later on. Its uses also extend to a steady flow of ingredients for non-food items, such as paper.

The simplest use of farming is to ensure you're never in short supply of food, thereby being constantly able to fill your hunger bar, even in the middle of the night when going off in search of a stray pig may prove fatal.

Here you'll find some of the basic recipes to get you started, as well as where to find the ingredients necessary to get you on your way, and a few other uses for the farming system which may benefit you later on in your game. You will also find some of the basics of animal farming here, which will prove useful for both food and wool harvests.

Note that while farming isn't essential to your progress, it will make your life a lot easier, particularly during the dark Minecraft nights when you don't want to be caught unawares while out scavenging to fill that all-important hunger bar.

"Farming will ensure you're never in short supply of food"

Lighting your farm
You'll want your farm lit up. Light is required for seeds to grow and torches provide it, even at night

Keeping land fertile
Though not required, keeping land fertile with water decreases the time it takes for plants to be ready for harvest

Tilling the land
Tilling land allows you to plant seeds, which will then grow until they are ready to be harvested

Crafting a hoe
This is your most important tool when starting a new farm area – it is used to till the land

Uses for farming

Here we'll share some practical uses for the farming mechanics

Farming will be your most reliable way to keep a steady flow of food – something particularly handy when night falls. Not only will it save you the trouble of looking for a wandering animal in the dark, it means you won't have to confront any Mobs while searching. This can be invaluable early on in the game when you have no armour.

Farms can also be used to grow sugar cane, which in turn can be used as an ingredient in paper, for creating books and maps. Tree farms will allow you to have a constant supply of wood for crafting or building, or even making

a giant tree house or watch towers, if you would prefer.

Players can also build indoor/underground farms dedicated to growing and spreading mushrooms. The mushrooms can then be used to create more food, or ingredients for potions later on in the game.

Rarer types of food for farming can be found by adventurous players – primarily potatoes and cocoa beans. Potatoes can be used to create baked potatoes; and cocoa beans, as well as being used as a key component for brown dye, can also be baked into cookies.

Key features

1: Renewable food
The ability to grow wheat and breed animals means you are never going to go short of food in the middle of a busy night. Making bread, cooking steaks and even baking cakes can fill your hunger bar in emergencies.

2: A steady supply of wool
It may seem a small thing, but wool can be used to create beds which will see you safely through a night. For the decorators among you, wool can also be coloured and used as a carpeted floor in your house.

3: Renewable energy
With a wood farm it's possible to harvest and then immediately smelt the raw wood blocks. The smelted wood will become charcoal – used to create torches for exploration and lighting, or to power a furnace for cooking and further smelting.

4: Making magic
Mushrooms can be used for more than just food. They are also an ingredient in potion making with a brewing stand. The sheer volume of mushrooms you can farm by using some bone meal makes them a useful resource. Mushrooms also naturally spread slowly in the dark, so be sure to farm them underground or even in a dark room in the back of your house.

"Farm mushrooms underground or in a dark room"

5: Animal breeding
Whether you want to do this for food or to simply have an army of animals, pens will allow you to breed sheep, cows, pigs and more to your heart's content. This means wool, food and leather are in constant supply. Basic armour, food and wool never came so easily. If you have the type of food the animal likes (eg sheep like wheat) and there are two of them, they'll kiss and create a baby.

Breed animals on your farm

Here you'll learn some of the things required to successfully breed animals

The process of animal breeding involves finding the kind of food the animal you wish to attract likes, luring it to your desired area and making sure there are two of them. Each animal likes a different kind of food, which will be detailed later on.

The food attracts the animal's attention and will get it following you. You can then lead it to your farm to prepare it for breeding. An enclosed pen is ideal, since animals have a tendency to 'miss' each other if too far apart. If you must have a bigger pen, prepare to spend some time forcibly shoving the animals into each other.

Once the two animals you require are in your pen, feed them each the required food and they will enter an 'in love' state, where they are ready for breeding.

Discover how to breed animals

1: Find the right food
In this example, we're going to find a sheep. We need simply hold a piece of wheat in our hand and get close. When the sheep notices, it will follow.

2: Luring to a safe spot
For simplicity's sake, have an enclosed pen near your home. Animals can have trouble 'finding' one another if they are too far apart, so the smaller the better.

3: Feeding the animals
Feed the animals their desired food – in this case the wheat – and they will enter an 'in love' state, where they are happy to breed with one another.

4: Rinse and repeat!
After two animals have a baby, they will need to be re-fed so they will once again be ready for breeding. A baby takes roughly five minutes to fully grow.

Attract animals to your farm

Each animal needs different food to lure it. Here's what they like and where to get it…

Minecraft animals are predictable creatures.
Fortunately, this allows us to easily make them our friends. Below is what you'll need to coax them into following you. Note that the food has to be currently equipped in your hand – just having it in your inventory will not work…

- Pigs will follow you for a carrot.
- Sheep will follow if you have some wheat.
- Horses will be tempted by a golden apple.
- Wolves can be led on by any kind of meat.
- Cats will come running if you have a raw fish.
- Chickens will be your friend for some seeds.

These foods must then be fed to the animals once they're in your pen. This lets them enter the love state where they are happy to breed. Whenever a baby is born, each parent will drop a small amount of experience and will need to be re-fed before they will breed again.

How to entice animals

1: Pigs and carrots
Carrots are available as a rare drop from Zombies. Sometimes villagers will have planted carrots which you can take – a slightly easier method.

2: Sheep and wheat
Wheat is the easiest ingredient to get a hold of. Simply break long grass to get your own seeds and plant them, or find a village farm and take some.

3: Horses and golden apples
Golden apples are rarely found in dungeon chests. An easier way is to craft them – surround a regular apple with gold ingots to make one yourself.

4: Wolves and meat
Any type of meat will do in this case. A wolf will follow for rotten flesh, if need be. To tame a wolf, however, a bone must be used.

5: Cats and fish
Unsurprisingly, cats will follow you for a fish. Craft a fishing pole and find a raw fish to lure a cat to your breeding cause.

6: Chickens and seeds
Seeds are easy to come by. You can either harvest them from village farms before they've grown or, more easily, punching long grass will yield them.

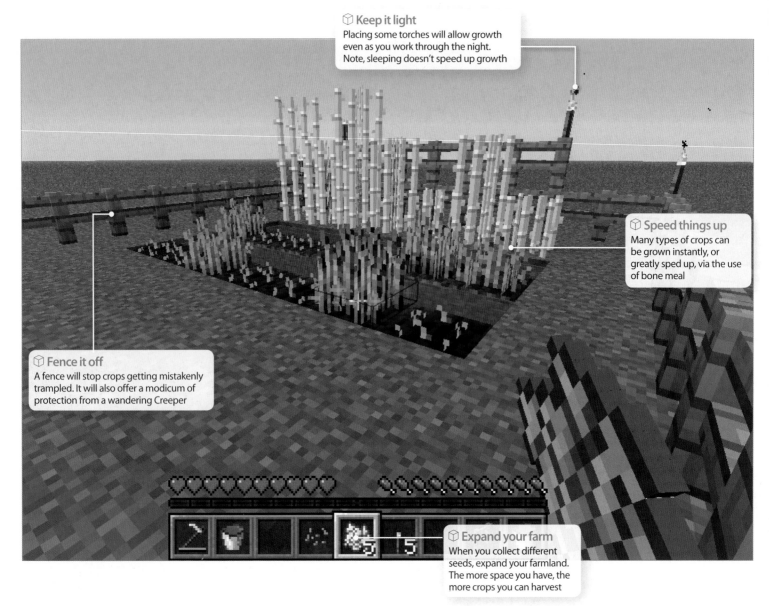

Keep it light
Placing some torches will allow growth even as you work through the night. Note, sleeping doesn't speed up growth

Speed things up
Many types of crops can be grown instantly, or greatly sped up, via the use of bone meal

Fence it off
A fence will stop crops getting mistakenly trampled. It will also offer a modicum of protection from a wandering Creeper

Expand your farm
When you collect different seeds, expand your farmland. The more space you have, the more crops you can harvest

Learn to grow crops

There are a few different types of crops available in Minecraft, from wheat to pumpkins

Growing different crops is where you will get your food from. With the different crops available, you can make anything from a simple loaf of bread to pumpkin pie. All foods restore a different value of hunger, but some are easier to find and produce than others.

To begin with, your farm will likely be covered in nothing but wheat. This will start you off nicely and, once fully grown and ready for harvest, will allow you to make bread or hay bales, which can feed your horses. As you progress you will be able to plant different seeds and crops, which will be detailed here.

To start your farm, all you require is a hoe (wooden will do), some seeds which you can get from breaking long grass, and the space to make it. Be careful around your crops, however: walking over them can trample them before they're ready to harvest, so be sure to leave some space to walk around them.

Preparing the land to grow crops

1: Preparing the land
Before you can plant anything you'll need to till the land, which can be done with a hoe. Simply right-click on grass/dirt blocks. Have water close by for optimal growth and you're ready.

2: Wheat
Your basic farm starter, wheat is grown from seeds that are found by breaking long grass. Once planted, the seeds will grow into wheat – which, when broken, yields the wheat itself and more seeds.

3: Pumpkin
Pumpkin seeds can be obtained by finding a pumpkin in the world and placing it into any square of the crafting window. This will give four seeds that can then be planted to grow more.

4: Melon
Melon seeds can be found in chests in abandoned mineshafts, or bought via trading with villager NPCs. Melon crops grow on the adjacent block from where they were planted.

5: Potatoes
Potatoes are obtained as a rare drop from Zombies, or NPC village farms. Each fully developed crop yields between one and four potatoes. Potatoes can be put into a furnace, resulting in a baked potato.

6: Carrots
Carrots are also found as a rare Zombie drop and from NPC village farms. As well as being eaten, carrots are used to lure pigs into your farms and fed to them for breeding.

7: Cocoa beans
Cocoa beans require a different method to grow. They can be acquired from, and planted/grown in, jungle trees. Each fully grown cocoa bean pod will yield three or four cocoa beans that you can replant.

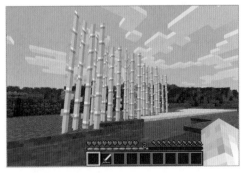

8: Sugar cane
Your best chance to find sugar cane is looking for sand surrounded by water. A single piece will grow three blocks tall. You can keep trimming the top two blocks, allowing it to regrow indefinitely.

9: Mix it up
Seeds of all kinds can be planted next to one another. Just be sure to make room for certain kinds, like melons, which grow on adjacent blocks rather than the one they are planted on.

Find and use mushrooms

Mushrooms growing in a dark place will provide plenty of food when required

There are two different kinds for making food with and a biome dedicated to oversized ones, but how do you grow mushrooms? Simply place them in a darkened room, which must be light level 12 or lower, far apart, and leave them to slowly spread.

A faster way to produce mushrooms is to use bone meal. So long as they're planted on dirt, grass or mycelium blocks, bone meal will turn a single mushroom into a giant, oversized version of itself. These can then be harvested for more mushrooms at a much greater speed than simply waiting for them to spread.

While the main use of mushrooms is to feed you, via mushroom stew, they can also be used as ingredients for the budding alchemist to create potions with a brewing stand.

The role of mushrooms

1: Finding mushrooms
Before you can plant your own, you'll have to find one of each kind. While they can be found in caves, it's easier to search dense forested areas underneath trees.

2: Making them spread
Mushrooms require very little light – too much and they'll uproot. A torch or two, five or more blocks above them should suffice. Keep them spread apart.

3: Make some stew
One red mushroom, one brown and an empty bowl will give you a bowl of stew. The ingredients can be put anywhere, so a crafting table is not required.

4: Make them huge
Using bonemeal on a red or brown mushroom will create a giant mushroom, if it has space to grow. These can be cut down to harvest more mushrooms.

Plant mushrooms

Once you've got mushrooms, you will need somewhere to plant and spread them

One of the more challenging parts of a mushroom farm is finding somewhere that will spread them effectively. If your farm is too light, the mushrooms will pop out of the ground.

One of the simplest structures to house mushrooms is an underground room, where you can control light and pick them as they grow. However, you can create a larger mushroom farm outside, provided they are shielded from sunlight.

While the popular method is to use bonemeal on mushrooms as a more efficient way of harvesting them, the steps below will help you create a very simple structure to house them underground. This can be built under your house. Just remember: naturally spreading mushrooms can take a very long time.

Top tips for growing mushrooms

1: Dig out your room
First things first – you'll need to dig out the space for planting. Create a stairway of sorts, about ten blocks downwards, then dig out a room. Ours is 9x7x4.

2: Set up your room
Mushrooms can grow on dirt, grass or stone. Here we've chosen dirt for flooring. Roughly in the middle, break one block in the ceiling and place a torch in it.

3: Plant your mushrooms
For this small farm, we've placed one brown mushroom in a corner and one red in another corner, leaving plenty of space for the mushrooms to spread outward.

4: Wait
Sadly, natural spreading is a very long process. After over an hour, we had grown an extra four brown mushrooms while the red one was still sitting all by itself.

Crafting overview

Learn how to get started and defend yourself

Crafting is where you will get most of your items from in Minecraft. With it you'll build tools to help you out, weapons and armour to defend yourself and more complexities as you progress.

Over the course of this section, we'll explain how to build the more basic tools you will need to survive, as well as what you should be thinking about crafting as you stay longer in the world. This will range from pickaxes for harvesting ores, to swords and bows to defend yourself throughout the harsh nights.

Tools, weapons and armour are built with a crafting table, which is a three-by-three grid of blocks. Materials placed in certain patterns will result in the desired item.

Don't worry about things being too complicated too soon. Most of the materials you will need to get started with surround you when you begin the game. Eventually, however, these tools will become useless as you try to gather rarer materials, for which stronger tools are required.

Once you have ensured your continuing survival, you can then focus on some of the more complex crafting Minecraft has to offer – this includes railway systems and basic mechanisms through the use of redstone.

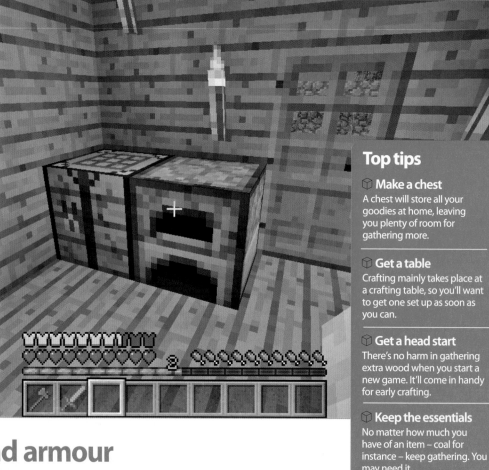

Top tips

Make a chest
A chest will store all your goodies at home, leaving you plenty of room for gathering more.

Get a table
Crafting mainly takes place at a crafting table, so you'll want to get one set up as soon as you can.

Get a head start
There's no harm in gathering extra wood when you start a new game. It'll come in handy for early crafting.

Keep the essentials
No matter how much you have of an item – coal for instance – keep gathering. You may need it.

"Tools, weapons and armour are built with a crafting table"

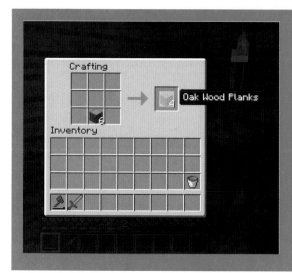

Why craft?

Crafting is important, but why the need to do it?

Crafting is how you'll assess your progress. With Minecraft's non-linear game world, your biggest indication of progression will be through the advanced tools, weapons and items you can make with the rarer ores and materials you find.

It will also serve to make your life an easier one. It's a tough job to punch the side of a mountain for hours to make a man-made cave, and it is made much easier with a pickaxe. If you want a door for that cave, you'll need wood; that's where an axe comes in handy. Should you want to set that door to open

when you press a switch on your wall, you'll need to get to work with redstone. No matter how simple the task, it will likely be easier through crafting.

Once you've mastered the basics and spent some time getting comfortable with the crafting table and the ingredients you can find throughout the world, you can move on to more advanced items. These can range from better weapons and armour to utility items, such as minecarts – to either move yourself about faster or set up a production line in a cave you are currently exploring.

Key features

1: Speed things up

Punching down your first few trees is a chore. Fortunately, this can be quickly remedied with a handy wooden axe. Not only is it made of the tree you previously punched down, it will make the next tree you fell come down quicker.

2: Convenience

An important part of Minecraft is your home, or base. With the crafting tools available, you can outfit your home with items that will make life easier, be it a crafting table or furnace, or a bed to automatically progress to the next day.

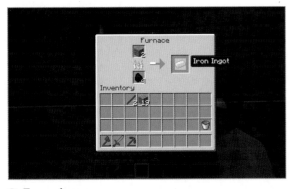

3: Experience

While you won't get much, crafting a furnace and smelting/cooking with it gives experience to help progress your in-game 'level'. Every little helps and this is a reliable way to gain it early on when you may not be comfortable hunting mobs.

4: Utility

Tools and weapons are not the only things you can craft. For example, buckets can be made and filled with water, flint and steel can set things alight, redstone torches can activate mechanisms, chests can store excess loot. There are a great many more utilities you can craft that will help you on your journey, not to mention things you can place inside your home.

"Tools and weapons are not the only things you can craft"

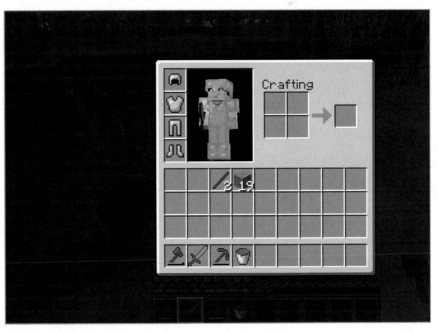

5: Defend yourself

Utility is great, but you won't get far without some protection. Crafting allows you to arm yourself with swords and bows, don protective armour and set traps. While you'll only start out with a wooden sword and no armour, quickly you will find yourself a formidable foe to any wandering mobs unlucky enough to cross you. While you won't be immortal, you will at least no longer run in terror if you see more than two monsters coming at you.

Top tips

Upgrade your gear
While wooden tools will suffice early, better gear can be crafted. From wood to stone will be your first upgrade.

Bring spares
There's nothing worse than being at the centre of the world and having your pickaxe break. So craft multiple items.

Know your tools
Always know what the tool you're using works with. It's a waste of durability to harvest dirt with a pickaxe.

Be prepared
Tools deteriorate with use. Keep an eye on the bar under the tool in your hot bar to see if you need a new one ready.

Understand the tools

You won't get far without some basic tools. You can punch down trees without an axe and get the wood, but punch a stone wall and you won't get anything – you'll need to use tools

When you begin a new game in Minecraft, you are given nothing but the clothes on your back. To get started you'll punch trees to harvest wood, but punching things will only get you so far. You'll need tools to progress: pickaxes, axes, hoes and shovels among them– to mine stone, harvest wood faster, till land and dig up dirt faster, respectively.

To craft any of these tools, you will also need a crafting table. This is made from four pieces of wood (not the raw logs), one in each slot of your 2x2 inventory crafting window. Once you have placed your bench and use it, you will see a larger crafting area, a 3x3 grid, which is needed to allow you to create these tools.

A pickaxe will be your best friend most of the time. It is used to break solid blocks of stone and harvest ore and it will likely be your most commonly used tool in the game. Certain ores will also need a certain strength of pickaxe. Wooden picks will harvest stone, coal and iron; iron picks will harvest redstone and diamond; diamond can harvest everything previously mentioned and obsidian. A gold pickaxe works the same as stone; it is much faster, but also very quick to break.

A simple wooden axe will fell trees faster than punching them and will come in handy when you need to chop down a lot of trees or pick up misplaced wood blocks.

Shovels will let you dig dirt fast, as well as digging up gravel properly; when dug properly, gravel has a chance to drop pieces of flint, too.

A hoe is used only for farming and even then only has one main purpose: tilling land. While it's wise to have one or two made, there's no need to keep them on your person. A better idea would be leaving them in a chest next to your farm.

Creating the basic tools

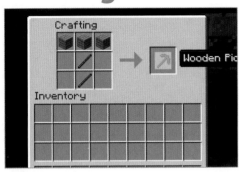

1: The pickaxe
Probably your most valuable tool, the pickaxe is made from two sticks and whichever material you'll be using. It is mainly used to harvest stone, coal and raw ore blocks from the world – and later, obsidian.

2: Different picks
Wooden picks harvest stone; stone picks harvest iron; iron picks harvest gold and diamond; and diamond picks harvest everything. Gold picks harvest stone, but have low durability.

3: The axe
Axes are used to harvest wooden blocks from trees. They are also used to chop down huge mushrooms. An axe is crafted from two sticks and three of the intended material.

4: Different axes
While all axes harvest all wood, the material used denotes the speed. Wood is the basic axe, followed by stone and gold, then iron and finally diamond. Gold axes are fast, but break very quickly.

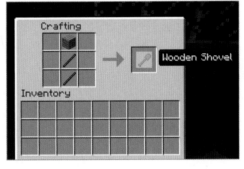

5: The shovel
Shovels are useful for flattening land for building. They are also used for digging up gravel, which can yield pieces of flint. You make a shovel with two sticks and one of your desired material.

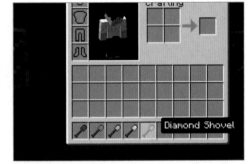

6: Different shovels
All shovels dig up all dirt blocks, but the material determines speed and durability. Wood is basic, then stone and gold, then iron, but the strongest and fastest is diamond. Gold is fast but breaks easily.

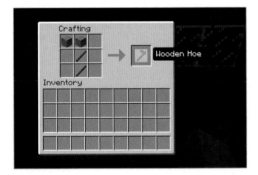

7: The hoe
A hoe is used to till land for farming. Right-clicking a piece of dirt tills it, ready for planting. Hoes are created with two sticks and two of whichever material you will be using.

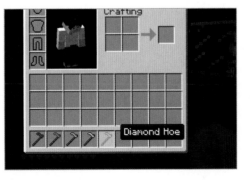

8: Different hoes
Unlike other tools, there is no difference in speed with hoes, only in durability. Wood is the least durable, then gold, then stone, then iron, and you'll see the most use from a diamond hoe.

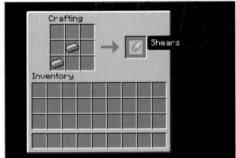

9: Iron shears
While not essential, shears are handy for shearing sheep. This doesn't kill the sheep in question and yields more wool than killing it would. A pair of shears are crafted simply from two iron ingots.

Protect yourself with armour

Weapons are good, but you'll also need some protection of your own from foes

Armour will keep you safe, but its importance when exploring underground can not be underestimated. It can mean the difference between getting home safely with your haul of mined goodies and one stray skeleton arrow making you lose it all.

It comes in different materials, each offering different layers of protection, measured by the armour bar above your hot bar. To get maximum protection from it, you must wear a helmet, chestplate, legs and boots. Leather will be your first armour set, which can be succeeded by iron or gold armour. These are followed by chain, which can only be obtained from mobs wearing it, or from trading with NPCs. Diamond is the best protection you can get yourself, but as you'd expect, you'll need a lot of it.

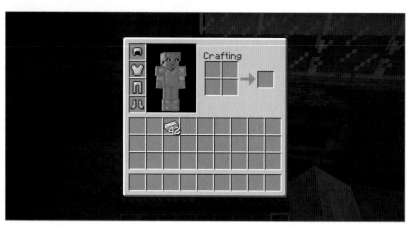

Build your own armour

1: The helmet
For this you'll need five pieces of the material you're using. Place your ingredients along the top of the crafting window, and the middle slot on either side.

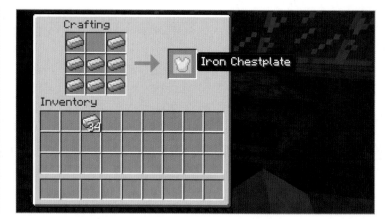

2: The chestplate
This is the most expensive piece of armour, costing eight of the material. Fill the entire crafting window except the top middle slot to create a chestplate

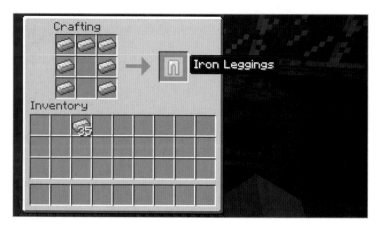

3: The legs
Covering your legs will cost seven pieces of material or ingots to make. To craft them, fill both outside columns of the crafting window, and the top middle slot.

4: The boots
These are the least expensive piece of armour, costing four ingots or material. Fill in the top or bottom two slots of each outside column to make them.

Create a map

There's nothing worse than being lost in the wilderness. Maps will help you get home

If you have ever spent some time wandering the world and realised you don't have a clue where you are, a map would have been your best friend. Not only can you follow a map back to the first point you used it, it shows you where you have been previously, meaning you can get on with exploring new areas instead of repeatedly ending up in the same spots.

Maps can be crafted as a standard version, or zoomed versions, which show more of the game world than the standard ones.

Once you have crafted a map and have it equipped (it must be your currently selected item, just having it on your hot bar does not work), right-click and it will draw the area around you. When you move out of that area, it will then draw your current path.

Get help finding your way around

1: Creating a map
To craft your first map you'll need eight pieces of paper (crafted from sugar cane) and one compass, which is made from a piece of redstone and four iron ingots.

2: Filling it out
You must have the map selected to use it. Once you move from the initial drawn part, the map will chart where you are walking. They aren't infinite, however.

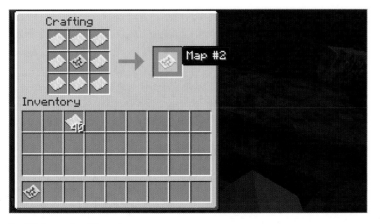

3: Make a better map
If you've filled your entire map, you can create a new, zoomed out one. To do this, surround your old map with eight pieces of paper at a crafting table.

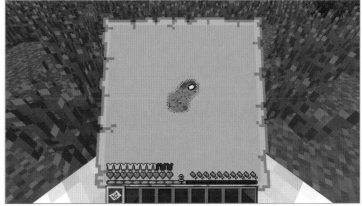

4: Zoom even further
Maps can be zoomed out up to four times. Repeat the process of surrounding your map with eight pieces of paper at a crafting table to zoom out further.

Build buckets

Buckets will allow you to transfer liquids from one source to another of your choice

Empty buckets are used to transfer the different liquids in the game – water, lava and milk. Whereas water and lava can be obtained from pools, milk is acquired by holding an empty bucket under a cow or Mooshroom and right-clicking. When filling buckets with lava or water, only full pools work; shallow, running streams will not work. Water can be placed around farms to hydrate the land, as well as being a useful tool for extinguishing fires. Any placed water can be retrieved by right-clicking on the source block. Lava is used as either a method to create obsidian (mixing it with water) or to fuel furnaces, which is the longest-lasting fuel in the game. Once you have placed a bucket of lava in a furnace, you can immediately retrieve your empty bucket.

Get help transporting liquids

1: Crafting a bucket
A bucket is made from iron ingots. To craft one, place the ingots in the positions shown above. Buckets don't stack, so be sure to have room for more than one.

2: Obtaining water and lava
To get water or lava, you'll first need to find some. Water is found above ground, but lava is rare there. It is more common deep in caves or mines.

3: Uses for milk
If you want to bake a cake, you'll need milk. A more important use is to drink it. This will cure you of any poisons you have been infected with.

4: Portable breathing apparatus
An odd use for a bucket is as an underwater breathing apparatus. Swimming forward and right-clicking will create a block where you can breathe.

Craft useful tools

Weapons and armour are all well and good, but everyone needs a little extra help

Crafting in Minecraft isn't just all about weapons, armour and tools to help you build or dig. Items exist that will help you with miscellaneous tasks, such as shifting liquid or keeping track of where you are and where you're going. There are also items you'll want to craft that will in turn help you with other items, such as enchantment tables and anvils. These can be used when required instead of carried. Two of the most often-used tools you can get are on the following pages, but here we'll show you some of the others that, while not essential, will still help you out in certain situations. The materials required to make them as well as the recipe and a brief description will follow, which will give you an indication of how these tools work and their purpose.

Get a helping hand

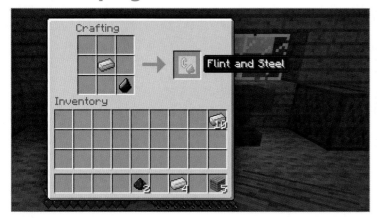

1: Flint and steel
This item is used to set fires wherever you see fit. A more practical use, however, is setting animals alight with it to make them drop cooked meat.

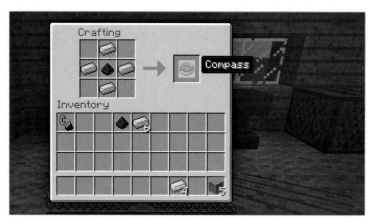

2: A compass for the lost
A compass will lead you back to your original spawn point – handy when exploring. To make one you'll need four iron ingots and one piece of redstone.

3: Keep track of time
A clock is the only way to tell the time underground and saves you re-surfacing in the night. Four gold ingots and a piece of redstone will get you one.

4: Sail the seas
To explore the sea, you'll need to craft a boat. To make your very own seaworthy vessel you will simply need five wooden planks, as shown in the image above.

Arm yourself with weapons

While you are digging and harvesting, every so often you'll need to defend yourself

Weapons will become a mainstay in your inventory early on. Coming across your first mob can be terrifying in the middle of your first night when armed with no more than a few blocks of wood. Fortunately there are a few weapons you can craft to even the odds. Here we'll outline how to make them. Whether you're a close range swordsman or a ranged fan of the bow, we've got you covered. As you progress you'll go from wooden weapons to more deadly, durable kinds where the Creepers and Zombies won't know what hit them. While you can enchant them to improve them, to get you started we'll focus on how to make the weapons. You will need a crafting table to make each of the weapons – your inventory crafting window is too small.

Building weapons

1: Strike with a sword
For close combat, swords are made from one stick and either two wooden planks, cobblestone, gold, iron or diamond – the best but most expensive.

2: Distance with a bow
Ranged combat is great against Creepers. A bow can only be made from wood: three sticks and three pieces of string, looted from spiders or breaking cobwebs.

3: Arrows for the bow
Having a bow can save your life, but it won't do much good without anything to shoot. Arrows are crafted from one stick, one piece of flint and one feather.

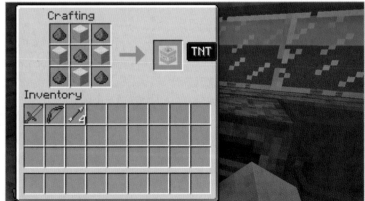

4: Some explosive fun
TNT can be made and set as a trap, or placed and set off in the heat of battle. To make some, you'll need four sand blocks and five gunpowder.

Use the weapons in your arsenal

Swords and bows may be easy to make, but how do you best use them?

So you are sitting in your house, crafting or redecorating and all of a sudden you need more wood. You grab your trusty sword and axe and head out, only to be surrounded by Creepers and Zombies, and Skeletons are shooting at you. Instead of flailing wildly at them, you could wisely use your different array of weapons. Here we'll go over the special uses each weapon has and how to set up a basic TNT trap that won't kill you.

Your sword should be used primarily against Zombies, and if you have an iron sword or better, Creepers. An iron sword should see them off before they get a chance to explode. Bows should be used against Skeletons so you can sidestep their own arrows, and against Creepers to try to take them out before they get in close.

Put your weapons to good use

1: Jump and swing
Your sword has good attack power, but you can improve it by jumping and then swinging. Connecting this way will score you a critical hit, dealing more damage.

2: Pull the string
Your bow can do extra damage. Instead of clicking the mouse button, hold it to draw your bowstring and then release the arrow for more damage.

3: Sharpen your swords
Swords can be made from multiple materials; wood is the weakest and diamond the strongest. Upgrade to better materials as and when you can for extra power.

4: A TNT trap
A TNT trap will see off any foes. Try placing the TNT underground and attaching it to a pressure plate on the surface, using some redstone to connect it all.

Keep it light
An important factor in any base is light. If it's too dark, mobs can spawn inside at night, both normally and while you sleep

Think ahead
While you won't get everything right away, think ahead and make space for items you'll make later to be placed

Get the basics
Any home should have three things: a crafting table, a furnace and a bed. Make sure these are the first things you place

Getting prepared
It's wise to gather materials before outfitting a base. Get a plentiful supply of wood, coal and cobblestone to start

Set up the ideal base

Your home base is without doubt your most important building in any game of Minecraft. It's where you'll sleep at night, craft, cook and more. As such, it's important to outfit it with utilities accordingly

Your house or base will likely start off as a box made of wood, barely able to fit a crafting table and yourself. As you progress, however, your base will grow, and you will be able to fit more items in there, both important to progress and to improve your quality of life.

While we won't tell you precisely how to make your base – that's left to your own discretion – we will show you some of the things you should highly consider including in there. These will range from necessities such as crafting tables and furnaces, to things you don't need but may very well want to

have – like enchantment tables, or anvils for repairing your gear.

Of course you will also need somewhere to store all your precious loot, so we'll also be going over how to create a couple of different kinds of chests to store items, as well as the materials needed to make all of it possible.

Please note: the items you can place in your base can require some rare materials to craft, so don't expect to have a base fully kitted out in a couple of in-game days. Half the fun is finally finding required parts and placing and using your item after a long

search, so don't fret if you can't make these things right away.

To begin, your crafting window will be in your inventory – a 2x2 grid, no use for anything complex. Once you have made a crafting table you'll have access to a 3x3 grid, which will allow you to craft everything, if you have the required materials. To make the crafting table, simply get one raw piece of wood, place it into any square of your inventory 2x2 grid and it will create four planks of wood. Put one plank in each of the 2x2 grids squares and you'll have your crafting table and be on your way.

Building what you need

1: Make a furnace
This should be the first thing you make after a crafting table. It allows you to smelt ore and cook food. It is made easily from eight pieces of cobblestone placed in the pattern above.

2: Beds for sleeping
A bed will let you skip the night and awaken the next day – very handy. You will need three pieces of wool, which is sheared from sheep, and three wooden planks to make one.

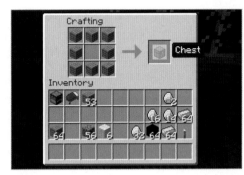

3: Chests for storage
There are a couple of different kinds of chest, but the basic one is the easiest to make. All you need is eight wooden planks around the outside of the crafting window, as shown above.

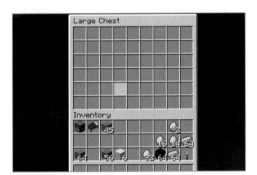

4: Double your storage
A chest is good, but it's also small to begin with. You can double your storage size in one place by simply creating another chest and placing it on the block next to your original one.

5: Fence yourself off
A fence around your base, well lit, will go some way to keeping it mob-free. Ordinary wooden fences are made with six sticks, which will get you two pieces of fencing to place around the base.

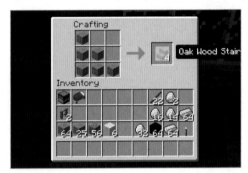

6: Step up
To save yourself having to jump up your stairs, make a set of steps you can walk up instead. To do this, place six pieces of cobblestone, wood, sandstone or brick in the pattern above.

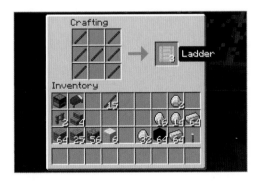

7: Up the ladder
As you'd expect, ladders allow you to climb up or down, useful for roof access or basements in your home. To craft them, you will need seven sticks, which gets you three pieces of ladder.

8: Anvils for repairs
Anvils let you repair items, rename them and enchant them with books. This useful item will cost you three blocks of iron and four iron ingots, so in total you will need 31 iron ingots.

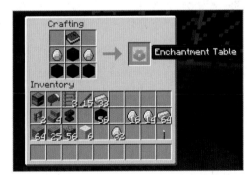

9: Enchant your gear
An enchantment table uses accrued experience to grant enchantments to weapons and armour. To get your own, you will need two diamonds, four obsidian blocks and one book, as above.

Fill your walls
Paintings and wall displays for items can be used to decorate your walls, giving it a more homely feel

Seal your house
As well as a door, a fence gives an extra layer of security as well as a nice decorative effect

Natural light
Nobody likes a sealed box. Make some windows for your walls to let in natural light during the day

Craft items to decorate your home

All the wonderful stuff you can build in Minecraft can leave your home or base looking a tad spartan. Sometimes it's nice to craft some decorations to spruce up the place

While decoration in Minecraft is a personal thing, there are in fact one or two essentials you will need while doing it. A snazzy painting and a weapon on display are all well and good, but will the painting or wall hanging save you from the Creeper who just walked in because you forgot to give your house a front door?

Or even better still, if you think physically pushing that door open is too much like the normal world, you can place a lever on the wall next to it to open and close the door. Or, for the super lazy, you could put down a pressure plate in front of it and then

you won't even have to right-click anything to enter your house.

As your home gets bigger, you will need bigger things to decorate. If you have a spare room that isn't seeing much use, why not craft a lot of bookshelf blocks and turn it into a library? For an added bonus, place your enchantment table inside that room; this allows you to use more levels of experience when enchanting, if the table is surrounded by bookshelves, and leaves a nice graphic effect.

Minecraft is filled with decorative ideas like this and once your imagination gets going you'll be

mixing old items with new ideas all the time. Hay bales or steps can be used for thatched and stepped roofing respectively, and glass panes can be crafted as windows, as well as glass blocks, if you want your house to have sunlight.

From the useful to the purely cosmetic, there are a number of options available to you. Some decorative items, like vines and hedges, can be found in the wild, but we are going to focus here only on the things you can craft yourself. All materials that you are going to need will be mentioned and, of course, the recipe to craft the item in question.

Make your home your own

1: The front door
A very important decorative block, doors can be made of either six wooden planks or iron ingots in the pattern above. Note, iron doors must have a pressure plate or lever to open and close them.

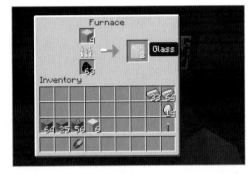

2: Glass blocks
Glass blocks are acquired by smelting sand blocks. One sand block smelted will yield one glass block. Be aware that breaking a glass block will not give you it back, so place them carefully.

3: Glass panes
These are very handy when making windows. They are made using six glass blocks and will give you 16 glass panes. As before, you can not pick them up once broken, so place with care.

4: Carpet your floor
Wool can be obtained by shearing sheep. It can then be dyed to your preferred colour and placed as flooring. The colour of the wool will not affect beds – they are always red by default.

5: Moss stone
This is tricky to get, as it is only available in dungeons or jungle temples, but it can be a nice change from standard stone houses, or even just around the frame of your house.

6: Liven things up
A jukebox lets you play music discs, which are found in dungeons or loot if you get a Skeleton to kill a Creeper. To make one, you will need eight wooden planks and one diamond.

7: Learn a little
Bookshelves enhance enchantment tables' abilities, as well as making for a good library-type room. To make one you'll need three books and six wooden planks, arranged as shown above.

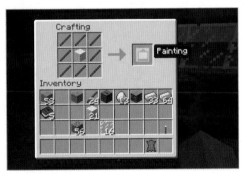

8: Add some art
Placing a painting gives you a random pixellated image. You can keep knocking them down and replacing until you get one you want. For your own, six sticks and one wool is what you'll need.

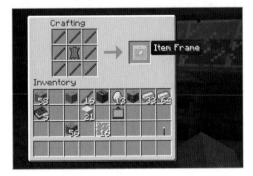

9: Show off
If you have an enchanted weapon you're proud of, or an item you really like, an item frame lets you display it proudly on your wall. To make one you'll need six sticks and one piece of leather.

A guide to mobs

Discover the friends and foes in Minecraft

Mobs in Minecraft are the non-playable characters that you will come across in the game world. There are both friendly and hostile Mobs, with the former including pigs and villagers; the latter, Skeletons and Creepers.

Friendly Mobs have a variety of uses, from providing useful items like wool to breeding farms of animals and trading items. Many Minecraft players construct farms to house chickens and pigs, for example. If you manage to find a village, you'd do well to trade with villagers for some rarer items.

Hostile Mobs, meanwhile, are each dangerous in their own right. Some, like Endermen, rightly instil fear in a player as they can cause a very swift death. Others, like Creepers, are relatively easy to defeat but their self-detonation ability can be incredibly frustrating. Still, hostile mobs – like friendly ones – are also useful as they drop specific items when killed.

However you approach your game of Minecraft, you will at some stage become involved with mobs for better or worse. In this section we'll ensure that you know how best to tackle each creature you encounter.

"You'd do well to trade with villagers for some rarer items"

Friendly spawning
Friendly mobs usually spawn above ground on grass or in wooded areas, although villagers only spawn in villages

Enemy spawning
Hostile mobs tend to spawn in dark places, either underground at any time or above ground when the sun has set

Characteristics
Understanding how different mobs behave is important to surviving and living in Minecraft, so brush up with our guide

Catching fire
Some hostile mobs burn in sunlight, while others do not. Knowing which do or don't can be useful for defensive purposes

Utilising mob drops

Learning what each mob drops is essential in Minecraft

Each Mob in Minecraft, be it a friendly one or a hostile one, drops some form of item that can be of use to you. Some mobs drop rare items that you won't find anywhere else, so it's useful to learn what each mob drops to obtain some of those harder-to-get items.

At first, fighting and defeating hostile Mobs may seem a daunting task, but as you acquire more ores from mining and create new items, you'll be able to beef up your defence and your attack, enabling you to venture outdoors at night and fight hostile mobs to acquire their item drops.

Each hostile mob drops items at varying rates. For example, a Creeper will drop between zero and two lots of gunpowder when it is killed. Hunting mobs can be very useful to acquire new items for crafting.

Friendly mobs also have useful items that you can learn how to make the best use of. For example, while a sheep drops wool when killed, you can shear them to get their wool instead of killing them, so that the sheep doesn't disappear from the game world.

Know who drops what and you'll be on your way to success.

Mob: Creeper

These infuriating mobs can also be one of the most dangerous foes you'll encounter

There's nothing worse in Minecraft than having a Creeper sneak up on you and, before you can move to a safe distance, it explodes and leaves you all but dead. Yes, Creepers are walking time bombs, and they are one of the most annoying mobs to encounter.

Creepers are one of the most iconic mobs in Minecraft, and they have become the game's unofficial mascot of sorts. They are easy to outrun but will attack you even if they are not provoked. Of course, their only form of attack is self-detonation, but it can take off 24 hearts, or 48 if they are charged by a rare lightning strike.

These mobs spawn during the day and in light conditions lower than seven, so you'll likely encounter them fairly frequently, especially as they don't catch fire in sunlight like other mobs.

Creeper features

1: Silent but deadly
Creepers only make a shuffling noise, or sound like a burning fuse when they begin to detonate. Keep your eyes and ears open.

2: Attack over defence
While easy to defeat, Creepers have a deadly self-detonation attack that will severely damage you and surrounding structures.

3: They can be useful
Creepers drop two rare items: gunpowder and music discs. The latter, though, are only dropped if they are killed by a Skeleton.

4: How to fight them
A Creeper will enter self-destruct mode when it is struck, so the best thing to do is hit them and then back away at a safe distance from the ensuing explosion.

Mob: Spider

Although not the deadliest of mobs, spiders can still be dangerous in their own right

Spiders in Minecraft are notorious for their hissing noise, which you will no doubt hear a lot of the time, and their jumping motion that can see them pounce on you in a flash. Fortunately, while they can be rather tough to beat, they cause little damage to the player. One of the major benefits is that they drop string, which can be used to make a variety of things including wool and fishing rods. On rare occasions they also drop spider eyes, which are useful for brewing potions.

Aside from the regular spider, there are two other types you should look out for. These are the Cave Spider and the Spider Jockey, the former being a poisonous variant of the regular spider while the latter has a Skeleton riding on the back of it, adding ranged attacks to the spider.

Be wary of these arachnids

1: Recognisable hiss
The unmistakable hiss of a spider can often be heard even when it is not in sight. It's a good indication of where a spider is.

2: How they move
Spiders can cover two to three blocks with each jump, but you can easily outrun them. Be warned, though, that they can climb heights and scale walls.

3: How to attack
Spiders are sometimes found in groups, so be wary when attacking. Spiders can't enter spaces that are one block wide, so use this to your advantage.

4: Their behaviour
Spiders will attack even when unprovoked and do not catch fire in daylight. They can also see you through solid objects, so they can track you even underground.

Mob: Skeleton

The ranged attacks of these mobs make them particularly dangerous

Many of your deaths in Minecraft will likely be caused by Skeletons. They can attack from distance with their bow and arrow, making them a formidable opponent. Indeed, when on your last legs, there is nothing worse than coming face to face with a Skeleton.

Their bow can cause between one and three hearts of damage, although they themselves only have ten hearts of health. Defeating them can be a case of running up close before they can inflict too much damage, or attacking from distance with a bow of your own. It's best to approach a Skeleton with armour on.

Skeletons burn in direct sunlight unless in shade or water, which they will often attempt to find before the sun comes up. Some Skeletons can also pick up armour, making them especially difficult to beat.

A bony foe

1: Useful Skeleton drops
A Skeleton drops between zero and two arrows and bone upon death. The latter is especially useful as it can be used to make bonemeal.

2: Beware the ranged attack
Skeletons have a bow and unlimited arrows, so will continue attacking you from distance if they can see you. Defeat them quickly to avoid considerable damage.

3: Looking out for Skeletons
Skeletons have a noticeable rattle. They will chase after you, and can even climb stairs to get you. They can be easily outrun, although their arrows cannot.

4: Enchanted item drops
On rare occasions a Skeleton may drop an enchanted bow or armour, which will have added benefits compared to the regular items.

Mob: Zombie

The most common hostile mob, fortunately they're not too tough

While exploring the world of Minecraft you'll come across Zombies more than any other mob. They spawn in dark areas and will attempt to damage you by shuffling towards you and hitting you. They emit a noticeable groan, so spotting one isn't too difficult. Like Skeletons, Zombies catch fire in sunlight so you don't have to worry about them during the day. They have ten hearts of health and cause between one and four-and-a-half hearts of damage, depending on their difficulty.

Zombie Villagers are the same as regular Zombies except for their heads, which are undead versions of villagers. Some other Zombies can spawn equipped with armour and weapons, making them considerably more dangerous. Their drops aren't very useful, though, so spending time hunting Zombies isn't too important.

Understanding zombies

1: Groups of Zombies
Zombies spawn either alone or in groups of up to six, and although they're easy to beat, a group of them can still cause you damage if you're unprepared.

2: How they behave
As soon as a Zombie spots you it will come after you. They are adept at avoiding obstacles on their way to you, so be warned that they can be quite versatile.

3: Calling for help
Zombies can call for help when you attack them. This can see you quickly overwhelmed, so kill them quickly before they call more of their friends.

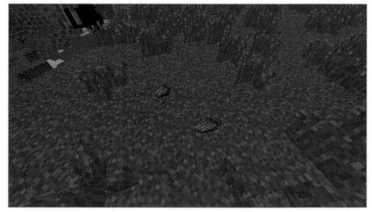

4: What they drop
Zombies can drop rotten flesh, carrots, iron ingots and potatoes. On rare occasions, though, they may drop enchanted weapons and armour.

Mob: Slime

This hostile mob is relatively useless but annoying all the same

Slimes are immediately noticeable for their large hopping motion across the world. They are easily outrun and defeated, but a large Slime will multiply into smaller versions when attacked, which can pose a problem. Slimes come in three sizes. As mentioned, the biggest will split into multiple smaller Slimes when attacked, while a smaller version will disappear when defeated. The bigger a Slime, the more health it has; large Slimes have eight hearts of health, while the smallest Slime has just half a heart. The former can cause two hearts of damage to you, but the latter poses no threat at all.

Like some other hostile mobs, Slimes spawn only in low light levels above ground and in swamp biomes. However, underground between levels 0 and 39, they can spawn in any light level.

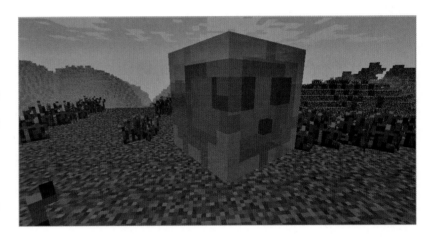

The annoying mob

1: What they drop
Tiny Slimes drop between zero and two slimeballs – useful for making sticky pistons, and can also be combined with other items to brew specific potions.

2: Attack and defense
Slimes attack by touching you and will deal damage relative to their size. Larger slimes multiply into smaller versions when you kill them.

3: Movement and behaviour
Slimes move by hopping, which they do roughly every second. If they spot you within 16 blocks they will hop towards you, but fear not as they are easily beaten.

4: Use them for experience
Slimes are useful to gain experience points. They are easy to beat and spawn in large numbers in swamps, so use them in this way to your advantage.

Mob: Ghast

If you venture into The Nether, be very wary of this hostile mob

Ghasts are particularly dangerous mobs that you will encounter only in The Nether (you can learn how to get into The Nether later in this bookazine) and they can be very hard to beat. These hostile mobs float through the air of The Nether and shoot fireballs at the player at a frequent rate, setting fire to both you or your surroundings.

With a size of four by four blocks, Ghasts are at least somewhat easy to hit with arrows, and with just five hearts of health they can be beaten. However, they can cause up to eight-and-a-half hearts of damage with their fireballs, in addition to setting you on fire.

You won't encounter them in the real world, nonetheless if you venture into The Nether you will at some point have to tackle these deadly mobs.

A mob from The Nether

1: Floats like a butterfly…
Ghasts float around the Nether slowly, but will search for a player within 100 blocks and attack within 16, making them very tough opponents.

2: …stings like a bee
Ghasts only fire when they can see you, but they will launch one fireball at a time, which explodes and sets fire to the surrounding landscape in The Nether.

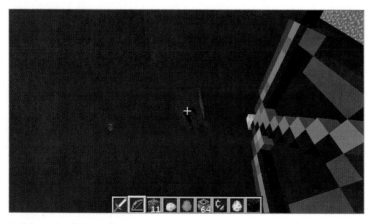

3: How to beat them
When a Ghast attacks you it will raise its altitude, so the best way to beat them is to use a bow and arrow, and make sure you've got a lot of armour as well.

4: What they drop
When killed, a Ghast drops between zero and two gunpowder or zero and one Ghast tears – a useful brewing agent. Ghasts often float over lava, though.

Mob: Blaze

These odd-looking mobs are found only in The Nether, but have a useful drop

One of the most difficult mobs you'll encounter in The Nether is the Blaze. Often spawning inside Nether Fortresses, they have a body composed of rotating sections surrounded by smoke. To make things worse, they can also fly and set you on fire.

Blazes have both ranged attacks and close-combat moves. For the former they will launch unblockable fire attacks at the player, which can kill you in no time at all. For the latter, they will cause less damage when you run up close to attack them.

The best way to defeat a Blaze is usually with ranged attacks, either using a bow and arrow or snowballs, which they are susceptible to. When killed, they drop invaluable blaze rods, which are essential items for brewing potions.

A difficult enemy

1: Dangerous ranged attacks
Blazes will fire unblockable attacks from a distance which can also set you on fire. This makes them especially deadly and hard to beat, especially in groups.

2: How to beat them
Charging a bow takes time, so a good tactic is to bring snowballs, which can cause three points of damage and can be thrown more frequently than arrows.

3: Movement and behaviour
Blazes can fly, but tend to stay on the ground when not attacking. Once they see you they'll fly up and attack, so be wary if you spot one in the distance.

4: Useful blaze rods
When killed, Blazes drop between zero and one blaze rods – an essential ingredient for blaze powder and therefore a key brewing agent for potions.

Mob: Endermen

One of the most terrifying mobs in Minecraft that every player should be fearful of

Upon spotting an Enderman, the common response of players is to scream in panic and quickly run for cover. While they only attack when provoked (easier than you might think), Endermen have a formidable arsenal of moves, including teleportation.

Endermen have 20 hearts of health and cause between four and ten hearts of damage depending on the difficulty. They can pick up blocks and are the only source in Minecraft for Ender pearls. The most notable feature, however, is that they attack if a player merely looks at them. At this point they stare at the player and emit a terrifying noise before teleporting in for a swift close attack, which can kill in a few blows.

Endermen are predominantly found in The End, but they do spawn in the Overworld from time to time.

A formidable opponent

1: Movement and behaviour
Endermen move slowly, shuffling about, and can pick up blocks. They will only attack you if provoked by being attacked or if you look directly at them.

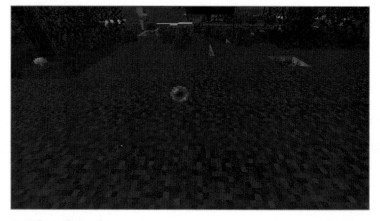

2: What they drop
Endermen are the only source of Ender pearls in Minecraft, which can be used to teleport players and also provide the only method to create an End Portal.

3: Where they spawn
Endermen often spawn in pairs in the Overworld, but one often teleports away. In The End, there are many groups of Endermen that can cause a swift death.

4: How to beat them
Vulnerable to water and rain, they can also be beaten by making sure you have the element of surprise, attacking them before they can respond.

Mob: Iron Golem

This mob can be a useful ally

In a sizeable village Iron Golems spawn naturally, with their sole purpose being to protect villagers from attacks from hostile mobs. Iron Golems are very strong, with 50 hearts of health and an attack strength of between three-and-a-half and ten-and-a-half hearts.

As you might have guessed, Iron Golems are made predominantly of iron. Upon death they will drop between three and five iron ingots. The chance of an Iron Golem spawning in a village is about one every six minutes, but they can also be created with a pumpkin or a Jack-o'-Lantern placed on top of four blocks of iron in a 'T' shape.

Iron Golems are loyal to villagers over players, but they are still useful. They will not attack the player per se, unless you provoke one by attacking it or if you attack a nearby villager. Iron Golems will also only attack hostile mobs within five blocks unless their village is under siege, in which case they will seek out and destroy any attacking mobs.

Mob: Snow Golem

Find out about these player-created mobs

Snow Golems are created by a player by placing a pumpkin on top of two blocks of snow, and they will be friendly to you once you've made them. They are, however, quite useless. They are weak, with only two hearts of health, and they can only cause damage to Blazes of the Ender Dragon. They can push mobs in the Overworld but, as you might imagine, this is not a great form of attack.

Snow Golems can not be created on a crafting table, so you'll have to make them in the world itself. When spawned, they will throw snowballs at mobs up to ten blocks away, but the snowballs do no damage. All they do is provoke the attacked mob. This can be quite useful, though, as Snow Golems do not necessarily follow the player, so they can be used as bait for certain types of hostile mobs. By having a row of them in front of your house, you can use them to push back incoming hostile mobs and keep your territory safe.

Mob: Horse

These tameable mobs can be used to traverse the world at great speed

Horses, one of the newest additions to Minecraft, are a very useful mob. Once tamed, you can place a saddle on them and they can be ridden around the world at a greater speed than walking. You can also put armour on them to protect them from attacks from hostile mobs.

There are a large number of different variants of horses in the game. The five types are foals, donkeys, mules, skeletons and undead, while many can have different appearances, allowing for a grand total of 35 breeds of horses.

Normal horses spawn naturally in the Overworld in groups of at least four. They are relatively rare compared to other passive mobs but, once found, you can tie them to fence posts (or hold them in pens) so that you don't lose them.

The benefits of horses

1: Taming a horse
Right-click on a horse with an empty hand to mount it. After being thrown off a few times, the horse will eventually allow you to stay on and control it.

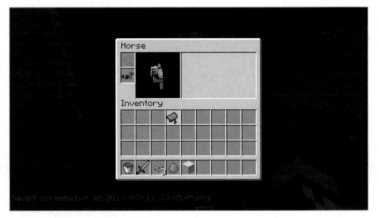

2: Equipping a horse
Horses can be equipped with armour and a saddle. The latter is required to control the horse, while the former is obviously useful when heading into battle.

3: Swift movement
Horses are great for fast movement in the Overworld. They can also jump quite high, making them especially useful for climbing large hills and mountains.

4: Breeding more horses
Feeding a horse a golden apple or golden carrot puts it into 'love mode', so it can breed with other types of horses and form offspring of varying types.

Mob: Wolf

These somewhat passive mobs can be tamed into a useful ally

Wolves are useful mobs that can act as a loyal companion to a player. They spawn in the forest and taiga biomes, and when they first spawn they are usually passive. If provoked, a wolf will attack a player. They drop no items, so there is not much point in killing them.

When they are wild and untamed, wolves have just four hearts of health and deal only one heart of damage with a close attack. However, when tamed, their health more than doubles to ten hearts, while their attack grows to two hearts. Taming wolves, therefore, is very useful.

Wild, hostile and tamed wolves can be distinguished by their appearance. Hostile wolves will constantly growl and have red eyes, while tamed wolves look less aggressive and have a collar around their neck.

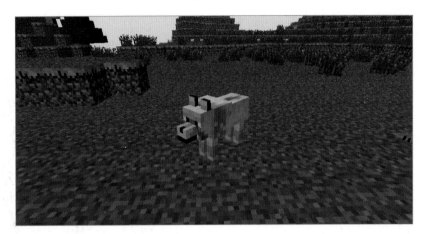

Taming wolves

1: How to tame them
To tame a wolf you need to feed it bones. Each bone has a one in three chance of taming it, with a maximum of 12 bones required to successfully tame it.

2: Man's best friend
Tamed wolves are often called dogs, as they are loyal to the player and attack enemies. There is no limit to the number of tamed wolves you can have.

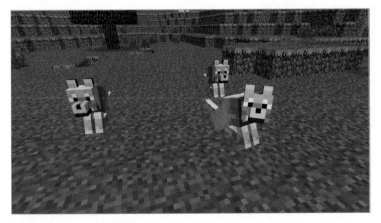

3: Actions with wolves
Tamed wolves will continuously follow you, although they can be told to sit. If you are very distant from the wolf, they will teleport to you if not sitting.

4: Useful in combat
Tamed wolves are great allies in combat. They'll attack any hostile mobs that could threaten the player. Using a pack of wolves is a good offensive strategy.

Mob: Pig

These passive mobs are a good source of food

Pigs in Minecraft mainly have one purpose: to be killed for their raw pork chops (which can then be cooked in a furnace). As you have to kill a pig to get its drop, however, it is wise to create a pig farm for a renewable source of food. They have five hearts of health but cause no damage as they have no attack move.

Pigs roam the Overworld in groups of at least three. They are not the smartest of animals and will often walk directly into obstacles (although not harmful ones) and even water, and can often be seen bobbing up and down. You can lead pigs with carrots, though, which is useful if you want to lead them into a pen.

If you have a saddle, you can also mount a pig and ride it using a carrot on a stick as a means of driving you forwards. They will eventually eat the carrot, but can gather considerable speed in the process. Plus, it can be a lot of fun riding a pig in Minecraft.

"You can also mount a pig and ride it using a carrot on a stick as a means of driving you forwards"

Mob: Chicken

Construct a chicken pen for a good renewable food source

Chickens, also called ducks, supply feathers, raw chicken and eggs, all useful items. They are slow-moving mobs with just two hearts of health and they sometimes attempt to fly over smaller objects. If trying to lure them into a pen, you can use seeds to entice them your way. Chickens tend to wander around with no purpose, although if they fall off a ledge they will flap their wings to survive the drop, while they also don't like being in dark places. They will sometimes try to swim, although they drown in water deeper than one block.

Upon death they may drop feathers and will always drop raw chicken. While alive, they will drop an egg every five to ten minutes. Eggs, when thrown, have a small chance of producing a baby chicken. So, you can create a self-sustaining farm of chickens to supply you with food, feathers and eggs. Adult chickens can breed by being fed seeds.

Mob: Cow

Use these passive mobs for useful items in the Overworld

Cows are larger than some other passive mobs. They are a bit tougher as well, with five blocks of health although, again, they have no form of self-defence other than running away. They are common in a variety of biomes and spawn in herds of at least four.

Cows can be held in a farm by putting them in a pen or attaching them to a fence with a lead. When right-clicked with an empty bucket, they will produce milk. When killed they will occasionally drop leather, but always at least one raw beef. As they can be milked indefinitely, however, it is good to breed cows and keep a few alive in your farm (if you have one).

They wander round the world nonchalantly mooing, and will walk straight off high cliffs by accident if they come across them. By giving them wheat they can be bred to produce baby cows, which again is very useful if you are trying to manage a successful farm.

"Cows can be held in a farm by putting them in a pen or attaching them to a fence with a lead"

Mob: Sheep

Seek out these mobs when surviving your first day

Sheep are incredibly useful, mainly because they are a primary source of wool. When killed they will drop wool, or they can be sheared to get wool and keep them alive.

Sheep have four hearts of health and spawn in a variety of biomes. Most are white sheep, but some are varying colours including black and grey, which affects the colour of the wool. You can also colour wool by using dyes.

Sheep are one of the least intelligent mobs in the game and will often walk straight into fatal hazards, including lava. They spawn in flocks of up to eight and can be heard bleating from a distance, so if you're struggling to find wool then keep your eyes and ears both peeled.

Like cows, sheep can be bred by feeding them wheat. It is useful to have some sheep in a farm, as wool is a useful item and it is better to shear sheep that are nearby than kill them, to provide a renewable source of wool.

Mob: Squid

These water-based mobs are a good source of ink

These passive mobs spawn in water and can often be found swimming around at depths from level 46 to level 62. They have five hearts of health and no form of attack, so they will always be passive towards you.

They have eight tentacles that they move when swimming around in water. They gather near lights underwater, which is a good way to attract them if you want to farm some of them.

Squid drop between one and three ink sacs, which are useful for making a variety of things, including dyes and a book and quill. Squid themselves have a fairly dull and black appearance, and in the darkness of water they can sometimes be quite hard to spot, so using a light is a good way to attract them. They can also swim against currents (except up a waterfall) underwater, and will swim away from a player if attacked. If exposed to air, a squid will eventually die.

"Squid themselves have a dull appearance, and in the darkness of water they can be quite hard to spot"

Mob: Ocelot

These cat-like mobs can be tamed as a pet

Ocelots are passive mobs that spawn only in jungle biomes. Like wolves they can be tamed, although they have no form of attack and only five hearts for defence. When tamed, they change their skin to look like a cat and will follow a player. To tame an ocelot you need to lure it close with raw fish, then feed it the fish. Cats are useful for one thing: scaring off Creepers. So keeping a cat close is a great way to fend off surprise Creeper attacks.

Ocelots themselves spawn on grass and will often be found in difficult-to-reach areas such as inside bushes. They are typically shy mobs with no form of attack, but they will spring away if a player makes a sudden or threatening motion nearby. Ocelots will attack chickens now and again, but otherwise are completely harmless. You should also remember that ocelots are scared of wolves and will run away, so it is hard to have both tamed with you at the same time.

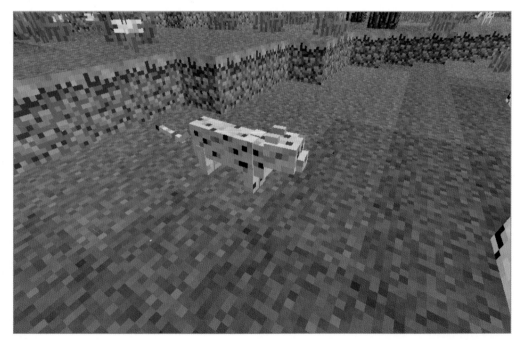

Mob: Villagers

These rather unique characters populate villages in Minecraft

Finding a village in Survival Mode can be incredibly difficult, but if you happen to come across one then you will also meet villagers. These passive non-playable characters spawn only in villages, and the varying types have different roles that can be useful to you. The characteristic appearance and noise of villagers makes them immediately noticeable. They randomly wander around and only interact with a player when asked to. The main purpose of villagers is trading. You can trade emeralds with them for a variety of items, based on their profession. The different types of villager are farmer, librarian, priest, blacksmith and butcher. Villagers randomly wander around and, with no attack, they will simply run away if you or a hostile mob attacks them. They are also able to use doors and houses in their villages.

Get to know the villagers

1: Finding a villager
Villagers only spawn in villages, which can be hard to find. If you do come across one, make sure you make a note of where it is so you can come back.

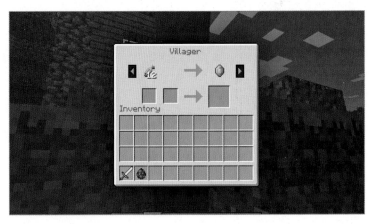

2: How to trade
When trading, they mostly accept emeralds as a currency – and as emeralds don't have any other use, you'll want to stock up on them to trade with villagers.

3: Breeding more villagers
Villagers will breed with each other, but only above ground in open space within a village. This spawns villager children, who grow up into proper adult villagers.

4: Different types
With five different types of villagers in the game, you'll want to make sure you trade with the right ones to get the items you're after, including things like paper.

Minecraft essentials

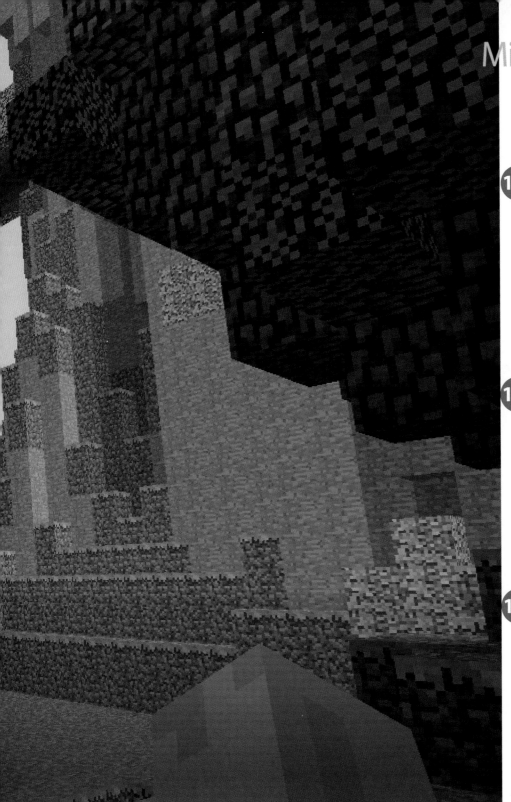

106

112

119

"Learn how to defeat the Ender Dragon"

Discover more in Minecraft

What to do once you've survived your first few nights

So, you've survived the first few days, gathered a few materials, and you might even have a small shelter that you call home. But what's next? There are no hard and fast rules in Minecraft, so really it's up to you what happens next in your world. However, we've come up with a few tips and ideas for things you might like to try, eventually culminating in the big boss battle that takes place in a realm called The End.

The depth of Minecraft really is astonishing, too, so there is a huge number of things you could try. Whether you want to create a kingdom for you to rule over or simply explore the almost endless game world is completely up to you. Over the next few pages, we've picked out some of the tasks and quests you might want to take on, the challenges associated with each, and the rewards you can gain if you're willing to put the time in. Whatever you want to do, our guide is the one-stop shop for everything you need to know about taking your game up a notch.

"We've picked out some of the tasks and quests you might want to take on"

Building
Creating your own, large house is a great way to express your creativity and build a base of operations

Farming
Whether you want to create a farm full of animals or create fields full of crops, you have the option to expand

Potions
Potions will give you a temporary boost to certain aspects of your character, which can be very useful

Enchanting
Do you want some more powerful weapons and items? Build an Enchanting Table and you can level things up

Going further, and going pro

Exploring the enormous game world of Minecraft

The world that is created when you start a new game is absolutely huge. In fact, on the PC and Mac versions of Minecraft, the world itself can generate infinitely, so you can walk in any one direction and never reach the 'edge' of the world. However, there's plenty to explore – the world is made up of all kinds of different biomes, including oceans, jungles, tundra and deserts. But that's not all: there's an underground world to explore, too, with mines hidden deep under the surface of the world filled with chests, rideable minecarts

and long corridors that often intersect with sprawling caves.

But the main world isn't the only one you can explore. An alternate realm, called The Nether, can also be entered once you've upgraded your tools and found enough of a mineral called obsidian to create a portal to transport you there. You'll need to go here if you also want to visit the realm called The End, which holds the game's final boss. That final mission will take a while to reach, with many challenges along the way, but it gives you a goal to work towards at your own pace.

Key features

1: Portals

You'll need a few hard-to-find materials to make a portal, but once it's built you can use it to dodge back and forth between the main game world and The Nether, making it a fantastic resource for you.

2: Building

Once you've mastered the basics of Minecraft, you'll be keen to build some more elaborate structures. Over the next few pages we'll show you how to construct impressive houses and add some flair to your dwellings.

3: Caves

Caves are a huge part of Minecraft. These naturally occurring holes can span for thousands of metres and lead you to all kinds of goodies if you're brave enough to explore downward… but you never know what else you might find down there.

4: Ravines/Chasms

These huge crevasses are dotted randomly around the game world and can catch out players who aren't watching their step, so make sure you're paying attention! As a bonus, though, they can often give you access to useful materials, so keep your eyes open as they can be of benefit to you on occasion.

"Ravines often give you access to useful materials"

5: Biomes

There are more than ten biomes to discover, and each has its own unique items, creatures and characteristics. Biomes are defined as regions that offer different geological features, helping separate the worlds into different environments. There are 12 main biomes that are covered elsewhere in this book, but you want to craft certain items, you'll need to explore them all to find their hidden secrets.

Create amazing structures

Nine ideas for creating an amazing base

Thanks to the huge scale of Minecraft, there is an almost endless number of structures you can build in your game world. And with every update, the designers add more and more blocks to the game. There are already plenty of options when it comes to creating a building, and the only real limit is your imagination. Coloured dyes help you change the appearance of wool, which can then be used to construct large images, patterned walls or designer floor coverings. Of course, you can also create large models using these blocks, or make a house shaped like something completely different.

Over the next few pages we've put together a few ideas for buildings you might like to try to create yourself, from large castles to small cottages and water-based boathouses. There are plenty of options for your base of operations and while it's important to choose the correct location for your house, it's possible to create a fantastic abode no matter where you spawn. So, get some inspiration over the next few pages, then start thinking about what you want to build first.

Tools of the trade
When you're building, excavating and clearing land will happen just as regularly as block placing. Make sure you're tooled up

Light it up
Make sure you light up your building as you go with torches, so you can always see what you're doing

Block collector
Make sure you pick up all the blocks you dig out where possible – you never know when you'll need a spare

Eyes on the skies
Keep an eye on the time; you don't want to get caught out and have monsters destroying your hard work

"It's possible to create a fantastic abode no matter where you spawn"

Building blocks
Get the materials you need

Before you start building, it's important to gather the materials you're going to need to finish the structure. When you're creating a house, the last thing you need is to run out of blocks for walls just as it's getting dark and therefore be attacked by monsters that appear at night.

It's also important to plan out what kind of building you want before you start; gather the blocks that you want to complete the full building, then mark out the corners of the buildings to make sure that everything fits together perfectly.

Using the right blocks is really important, too; make sure you've made glass by baking sand or you won't be able to create windows. Lighting is also important, so ensure you have enough torches or glowstone blocks to keep everything illuminated when it goes dark.

It's vital to consider the integrity of your home, too – if you make a house from wood it will be considerably weaker than a home made of stone, and is liable to set on fire if near a substance like lava. And, if a Creeper explodes nearby, you don't want your hard work being blown away – use a hard material to ensure it'll stay standing.

Begin building incredible structures

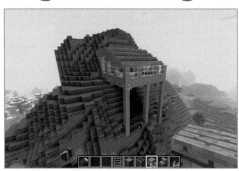

1: Mountain base
This hillside base not only offers a brilliant view, it also gives you easy access to the materials at the top of the mountain, and you can dig down to create a secure mine.

2: Brick house
This solid house will keep Creepers at bay thanks to the hardy brick walls. It looks great, too; the bricks are a little old-fashioned, but add a garden full of flowers and you've got a classic cottage.

3: Castle
If you prefer to show off a little more, you can create a castle featuring battlements, a drawbridge and even a moat. Cobblestone is a great choice here, giving a darker, more rustic look.

4: Boathouse
If you've spawned in a biome with a large ocean, you might want to build a boathouse off shore. This one features a jetty with a couple of boats, and a huge window for brilliant views.

5: Treehouse
If you're concerned about monsters, you might like a treehouse; in a jungle biome this is perfect, with amazing views and no threat from night-time creatures. You might not even need walls.

6: Farms
You can build farms around your house, too, to provide food and ensure you don't starve to death. Keeping them lit is important, and keeping animals out with a fence is also a good idea.

7: Bunker
If you have spawned close to a lot of large cliffs, or you find yourself in a ravine, a bunker is a great option. It's well positioned for mining, and very secure from monsters.

8: Glowstone
If you've made your way to The Nether you may have encountered glowstone. This brilliant block can be placed anywhere and emits light like a torch; perfect when building a house.

9: Skylights
No matter what kind of structure you're building, a skylight is a good idea. It gives light all day and allows you to see if monsters have spawned above you in the night.

Top tips

Mining
If you want to start a mine but your house is on a hill, consider starting your mine at the bottom – it will save you some digging.

Connections
If you have several areas around your house, you can connect them with underground tunnels to ensure safe passage.

Your kingdom
This place will be your base of operations and your kingdom, so choose somewhere with space to expand.

Location
Choosing the right location is very important, so make sure you choose somewhere with plenty of resources nearby.

Construct buildings

Top tips for creating a functional and beautiful structure in your Minecraft world

When you start building a new house in your Minecraft world, it's important to consider a few things. First of all, where you build is very important. Travelling across the world until you find a suitable place to build is a very good idea, even if it means you have to spend a couple of nights digging out quick man-made caves to survive the night-time monsters.

Once you find the perfect place, you can start building. Remember that the entire landscape can be altered, so there are plenty of things you can create to suit you. Whether you need a small home to serve as a camp for exploration or a base for extensive mining, farming or adventures into The Nether, you can create a brilliant structure with a little time and effort. Remember that the most important thing at first is shelter, so focus on getting your structure up, and then you can start customising it to your needs.

Everything you need to start building

1: Clear the area
Find an area you can use for your base and start clearing out the area. Any area can be terraformed to fit your requirements, so you shouldn't feel limited by a space that isn't immediately right.

2: Plan it out
Before you start building, climb up and look down over the area you've cleared. Decide where you want the corners to be, counting out the squares and building foundations before expanding.

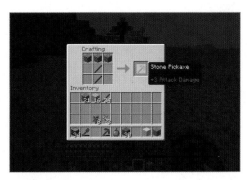

3: Tooling up
As you gather more materials, start upgrading your tools to make building and material gathering easier. Make sure you're using the right tools, too; a full toolkit of spade, axe and pickaxe is incredibly useful.

4: Light it up
As you build, ensure both the inside of the building and the surrounding area is well lit. Monsters can only spawn in the darkness, so if you light up the area around your house, nothing will spawn nearby.

5: Gather materials
If you want to build more than a basic house from cobblestone or wood planks, you'll need to gather more materials. Dig sand to make glass, clay for brick walls, and shear sheep for carpets and pictures.

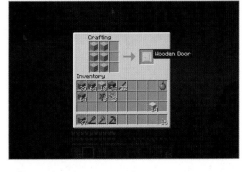

6: The mod cons
For some materials, like glass, you'll need to use a furnace. Others, like doors, can be made with basic materials. Place it on the outside of the building – it may seem obvious but it's an easy mistake to make.

7: Multistorey
Once built, start adding more to your building. Adding another floor is great for shooting enemies from high; place glass in each layer directly in line to ensure the light flows straight in.

8: Building a mine
If you want to keep expanding, you'll need the best materials, and to do that you'll need to start mining. Cover the top with glass for the best lighting and security, and build floors so you don't die if you fall in.

9: Underground city
As you expand, create tunnels to connect your various places. These offer much safer passage between, say, your house, mine and farm, than travelling over ground, especially during the night.

Lighting
It's important to consider lighting; this open ceiling allows daylight to come downstairs, while glowstone keeps things bright at night

Torches
Here we've added fence posts to the walls and put torches on top to create a more stylish wall lighting solution

Table
You can create this sunken table with fence posts, wooden slabs and wooden or stone pressure plates

Style
Work out the materials you want to use in your house based on what will add variety but also work well together

Upgrade your home

Don't settle for anything less than the best – these ideas will make your home into a mansion

When it comes to building in Minecraft, the first few days can often be a case of just getting by and surviving. Once you've had a chance to set yourself up, though, you can start to think about upgrading your house and making it more of a home.

There are loads of additional items you can craft that will help turn the place where you sleep into a home you are happy to come back to after a long day's exploring, mining and gathering. We've build a beautiful house and shown you a few ways in which you can create an incredible living space full of artwork, greenery, and chairs alongside the useful and vital equipment like crafting tables, chests and anvils. Of course, experiment with materials and find a style you like, but here are a few ideas for what you can do.

Add some finishing touches to your house

1: Foundations
While normally you would build on dirt, stone or other natural terrain, consider digging down a block and replacing the natural floor with something like wood for a more homely look.

2: Making an entrance
Place fence posts next to your door to create a small front porch, and use glass panes to form your windows. These are easier to see out of, and they look more like windows than normal glass blocks.

3: Water feature
An indoor water feature adds a touch of class. Here, the feature flows down the wall and then underneath the floor, with glass blocks giving you a view of the blue stuff from above.

4: Functional
Remember that your house still needs to be functional, too. Set aside an area, like here under the stairs, where you can work on making new tools, storing your belongings and cooking up food.

5: Make a bin
If you have loads of leftover cobblestone and dirt, make a 'bin' with lava gathered in steel buckets, but remember to surround it so you don't fall in, and keep it away from wood!

6: Sleeping quarters
Create some sleeping quarters, and consider using the new carpet blocks that were added in the 1.6 update to give your room a luxurious feel. A chest is a good idea here, too.

7: Very posh
Why not add a little art to your walls? There are a range of paintings to put up, and they are cycled at random so keep going until you find one you like. Bookcases look great, too.

8: Under pressure
One brilliant tip is to add a pressure plate next to any door. When you step on it, the door will open and close; it will save you a closing the door behind you every time you leave.

9: Landscaping
Don't forget the outside of your house, either. Why not add some flowerpots and these hay-bale plant pots (made with fence posts and leaf blocks) to give your garden some character?

An overview of The Nether

Going into the darkness is easier said than done…

One of the more dangerous expeditions you can undertake is travelling to The Nether, a world of fire and danger with huge lava lakes and enemies that aren't available anywhere else in the game. You might wonder why you'd ever undertake such a scary and difficult task, but the answer is simple – The Nether holds rewards that cannot be gathered anywhere else in the game. In particular, it holds items required for reaching The End, a realm within which a huge dragon dwells.

Getting to The Nether isn't easy, and once you're there you'll need to think fast if you want to survive. Over the next few pages we'll give you some tips and advice for getting there, surviving, grabbing the best materials and getting out alive. It's fair to say that The Nether is one of scariest parts of Minecraft, but entering it and fighting off the creatures it contains is also one of the most exhilarating things you'll experience in the game. So, tool up and get ready to enter the dark realm to reap the ultimate rewards…

Top tips

Lava, lava everywhere
The Nether is full of lava; it falls from the ceiling and forms into enormous lakes on the ground.

Enemies
There are all kinds of enemies in The Nether, including the peaceful-until-provoked Zombie Pigmen with their golden swords.

The tools
Make sure you have the tools you need before you enter The Nether or you'll be toast!

Fire burning
Small red blocks are called Netherrack. They burn forever, are great for decorative fires.

"The Nether is one of scariest parts of Minecraft, but exhilarating all the same"

Making the trip worthwhile
The blocks you can gather on a trip to The Nether

One of the best things about The Nether is the sheer amount of new enemies and blocks you will have to deal with. There are a few types of blocks that are only available in The Nether, so it's well worth grabbing them if you have the time and the tools. Soul Sand slows your movement and makes it hard for you or mobs to travel. This can make it an effective trap for enemies if laid in the Overworld. Netherrack is useful as a source of light, and as decoration; it's the perfect block to use if building a fireplace in your home.

The Nether also contains glowstone blocks, which are extremely handy when building. These blocks emit more light than torches, making them a valuable commodity. Mining them drops glowstone dust, and you'll need nine dust blocks to make another glowstone block. Finally, you can gather Nether Quartz, a material that can be used as a daylight sensor for redstone circuits.

Key features

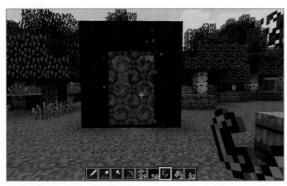

1: Build your portal

Once you've gathered some obsidian (and you can turn the page to find out the best way to do just that), you'll need to build your portal. The gap in the centre needs to be two blocks wide and three high, and lit with a flint and steel.

2: Portal options

Have you run out of obsidian? No problem – the game allows you to create a portal with just ten blocks of the black mineral. Simply form the portal in the shape shown in this screenshot and light it to travel to The Nether.

3: Achievement get!

Just as you enter The Nether for the first time, you'll get a small message appear telling you that you've unlocked an achievement. Well done! Don't get too carried away, though, as danger lurks on the other side of the portal.

4: Tooling up

Before venturing into The Nether, it's vital to check you have everything you need. Get rid of unnecessary or valuable items in case you die, but remember to take armour and weapons. A few spare pieces of obsidian and a flint and steel are a good idea, too, in case you get lost or your original portal is destroyed.

"Get rid of unnecessary or valuable items in case you die"

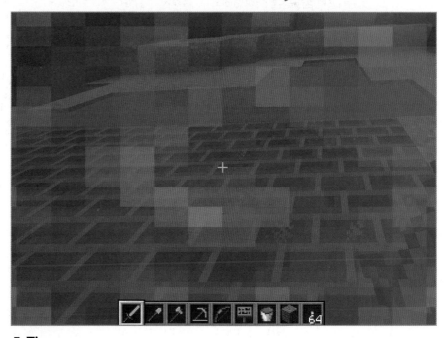

5: Time warp

Time elapses at the same rate in The Nether as it does in the outside world, but distance is very different. One block in The Nether is the equivalent of eight blocks in the Overworld. Therefore it's important to remember where your original portal was when you travel back so you don't return miles from your base. However, this does make The Nether useful as a short cut between two locations, despite its difficult terrain and hazardous enemies.

Fire!
A lot of blocks will be on fire, but they really just serve as light sources

Constant danger
As soon as you enter The Nether you'll be in danger. Ghasts will shoot fireballs at you right from the off

Prepare yourself
Before you enter The Nether, make sure you have everything you need and have stored valuable objects

Pointless water
There's no point bringing water into The Nether – if you place it anywhere, it will simply fizzle away

Find your way around The Nether

What to expect when you're heading into the darkness of The Nether realm

There are plenty of valuable rewards to reap if you're willing to take a trip into The Nether. From blaze rods to ghast tears, the items you can gather are well worth the trip as long as you are happy to take the risk. There are plenty of dangers to face if you're willing to enter The Nether realm, so you'll need to be extremely prepared for what you will encounter. Enchanting your items with advanced powers (especially fireproof armour and weapons with extra damage) is a great idea for giving yourself a good chance in The Nether. It's also very important that you equip yourself a with a bow and lots of arrows; there are plenty of flying enemies that will attack you on sight, and you'll need something to fight them off with. In these two pages, we'll detail some of the biggest threats to you while you're there, and the best things to grab on your trip.

What to look out for in The Nether

1: Magma cubes
These fire creatures behave a lot like Slimes found deep underground. They're hostile, jump every two-to-six seconds, and when attacked they split into four smaller versions of themselves.

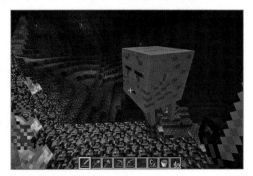

2: Ghasts
Ghasts are huge, flying enemies that will scream when they see you and start shooting fireballs. These can be deflected back with punches or arrows and if they hit the Ghast, will kill instantly.

3: Zombie Pigmen
Zombie Pigmen travel in packs, but are placid unless attacked. If you do choose to take them on, the whole pack will attack you and they'll do a great deal of damage, so watch out.

4: Blazes
These flying creatures spawn in groups and attack with fast-moving barrages of unblockable fireballs. They're difficult to fight, but a bow is your best choice as they can fly away if attacked with a sword.

5: Skeletons
You'll often find Skeletons spawn around Nether Fortresses. When combined with the other mobs they can be a real danger, so watch out for their arrows while battling Blazes and Wither Skeletons.

6: Wither Skeletons
Wither Skeletons will be found near Skeletons. They attack with stone swords and if hit, you may be infected with 'Wither', which will cause further damage. They may drop a Wither Skull when killed.

7: Blaze spawner
If you go into The Nether looking for a Blaze, you'll be happy to see one of these. These Blaze spawners are found in the Nether Strongholds and you'll need to be ready for three Blazes to appear at once.

8: Nether Strongholds
One of the main reasons to enter The Nether is the existence of Strongholds. You should be able to find one easily and they not only hold a great number of useful resources, they also make travelling easier.

9: Blaze rods
The biggest reason for coming to The Nether is to gather blaze rods. Dropped by Blazes, they allow you to form a number of useful items – including the Ender eye, required for travelling to The End.

Gather obsidian

Where to find the rare mineral you need,
and how to mine it

When it comes to materials in Minecraft, there is only one thing
tougher than obsidian, and that's the bedrock that stops you
digging through the bottom of the world. The black material
is formed deep underground when water meets lava, and if you
come across it, grabbing it is a good idea. It's the mineral you'll
need if you want to form a Nether Portal, and as such it's extremely
valuable. However, it's also incredibly difficult to mine; you'll need
the right tools for the job and plenty of time to dig if you want to
get your hands on even a single block of the black stuff.

Here, we'll take you through the best way to find obsidian
naturally, and how to get it once you've found some. Be warned,
though – this isn't an easy mission.

Find and excavate obsidian

1: Digging down
You'll need to go deep to find obsidian, and you'll also need to be lucky. The
mineral is only formed when water hits a body of still lava, so it's not common.

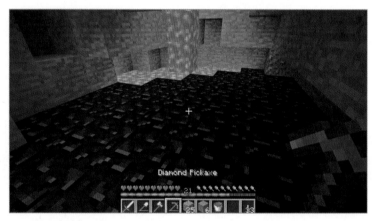

2: Found it!
If you come across lava, have a search for nearby water sources. However you
find it, you're going to need a diamond pickaxe to dig it up.

3: The long hard slog
Each block of obsidian takes about ten seconds to mine. You can enchant your
diamond pickaxe with an efficiency enchantment to reduce this, though.

4: Careful!
Beware mining obsidian that's formed in a natural lake of lava. There may still be
lava under the top layer, and if you or your block fall in you won't be happy.

Farm obsidian

Discover how to make your own obsidian on the surface

If you haven't had any luck with digging down to find obsidian, don't worry – all is not lost. There are other ways to gather the precious black stuff on the surface of your Minecraft world and while it might take a while to gather the materials you need to do so, in the long run it's probably quicker than travelling deep underground to find the mineral existing naturally.

First off, you may find a lava lake on the surface, ripe for turning into the valuable material by simply pouring a bucket of water over it. The manual method takes a little longer as it requires you to have many buckets in order to gather the amount of obsidian you need. Sadly, you'll need to gather multiple buckets, each one made of steel bars, and you'll need to have found lava for each of the buckets already.

Access obsidian on the surface

1: Create your farm
Create a hole seven blocks long. It's a good idea to make this out of something like cobblestone, and build it away from any trees or wooden structures.

2: Waterproof reeds
Add a small pool of water next to the channel, just in case you fall in and set on fire. Reeds will deflect water, so you can stand on this block safely.

3: Water it
Drop your water bucket on the stone block at the end of the channel, while standing on the reed block. When the water reaches the end, scoop it up again.

4: Mine it
Now you can dig up the obsidian you've formed. If you still have the buckets, go grab some more lava and you can repeat the process for more obsidian.

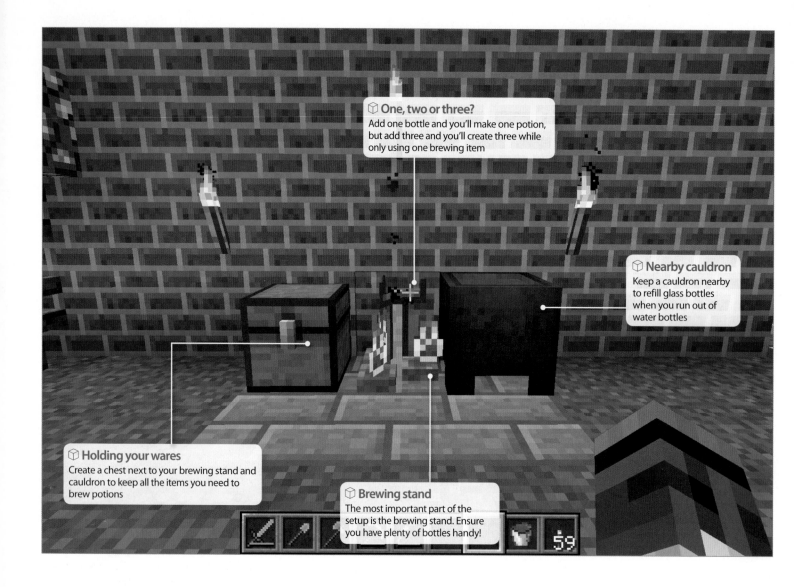

One, two or three?
Add one bottle and you'll make one potion, but add three and you'll create three while only using one brewing item

Nearby cauldron
Keep a cauldron nearby to refill glass bottles when you run out of water bottles

Holding your wares
Create a chest next to your brewing stand and cauldron to keep all the items you need to brew potions

Brewing stand
The most important part of the setup is the brewing stand. Ensure you have plenty of bottles handy!

Prepare to brew potions

Discover which items you need for brewing potions to give your character a boost

When it comes to powering up your character, you can craft armour and upgrade your weapons, but once you have all these accessories made of diamond, is that the end? Absolutely not. With the right tools, items and crafted materials, you can brew potions that give you new abilities and powers that can help when embarking on a new quest.

Admittedly, the items you need are really quite hard to come by, requiring trips to The Nether, journeys deep underground and some farming of certain foodstuffs. Still, if you want a slight edge when you decide to take on the Ender Dragon in The End, potions are the best way to do it.

In this tutorial we'll show you the basic equipment you'll need to create, and the four items that form the basis of all potions in the game. Then, when you're ready, turn the page to learn about some of the most useful potions you can create.

The ingredients for brewing potions

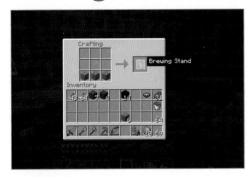

1: Brewing stand
First, make a brewing stand using a blaze rod and three blocks of cobblestone. You'll need to take a trip to The Nether to grab the blaze rod, so make sure you tool up before you go.

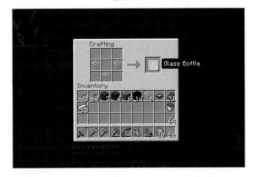

2: Bottles
You'll need plenty of glass bottles for your potions; create three of them with three blocks of glass placed in a V formation. You'll need a bottle of water for every potion you make.

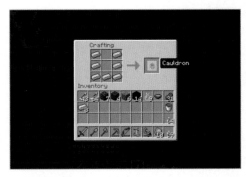

3: Cauldron
In order to fill your bottles with water needed for your potions, you'll need a cauldron. It is the only way to fill the bottles, so create one with a U-shaped steel creation.

4: Fill it up
The cauldron will spawn empty, so you'll also need to create a bucket and fill it with water, then tip it into the cauldron. If you remove the full cauldron, the water will disappear, though.

5: Filling bottles
Filling bottles is as simple as pointing them at the cauldron and hitting the right button on your mouse. A full cauldron will fill three bottles, so for big brewing sessions you might need refills.

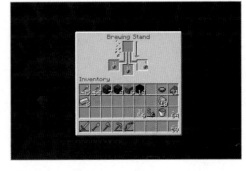

6: The brewing interface
This is the brewing interface. You'll need to add your water bottles in the lower three slots, then add the item used for brewing at the top. The arrow on the right shows the progress of the brew.

7: Full stand
Unlike when you leave items on a crafting table and exit the crafting menu, you can place up to three bottles in the stand and then walk away to gather materials. It can function as storage for potions, too.

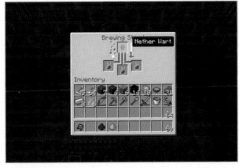

8: Brewing basics
There are four main items used to create basic potions: Nether wart, fermented spider eye, redstone and glowstone. These form the basis for the finished potions, for which you will need more materials.

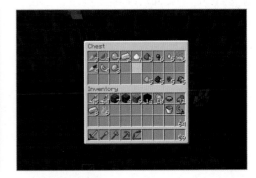

9: In the chest
Here, we've added all the possible items you can use for potion brewing into the nearby chest. Each item produces a different kind of potion, and some have the ability to intensify the effects.

Create potions

We take a look at nine of the most popular potions to brew

When it comes to giving yourself a boost, a potion is by far the best bet. Brew a potion from a few select ingredients and you can do anything from improving your healing speed to turning yourself completely invisible. They can offer real advantages when taking on certain quests, especially if you're taking trips into new, dangerous realms or going deep underground on a mining expedition.

The most important thing to remember about potions is that their effects are only temporary. Unlike enchantments, which will last for the lifetime of the item upon which you are putting a spell, each potion has a set duration. Once you drink a potion, all you'll be left with is an empty bottle and once your time for that potion is up, you'll need another if you want to feel the effects again.

Still, these recipes – combined with diamond weapons and armour and enchanted items – offer the very best chance when it comes to defeating the Ender Dragon. Spend time collecting the items you need to brew the potions, and check out the box below to find out how you can improve on basic potions to increase their effects, duration or power.

"The effects of potions are only temporary"

Top tips

Super effective
When you drink a potion, swirls of magic will start spiralling up from your body, showing its effectiveness.

In the armoury
Keep a healthy stock of different potions ready, just in case you need them in an emergency.

Long-lasting?
You can check how long your potion is going to work for by hitting the Inventory key.

Take your time
Each potion is a little like food – it takes a few moments to consume. Factor this in when drinking.

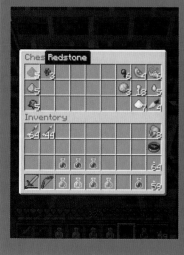

Primary, secondary and tertiary ingredients

Getting to know the items you'll need, and what they'll do

There are several ingredients you'll need for brewing potions, and they can be split neatly into categories. Primary ingredients are those that you can add to a water bottle to create what is known as a Base potion. These potions will do nothing upon drinking, and need to be brewed with a secondary ingredient in order to have any effect. There are four possible primary ingredients, and each one creates a different Base potion. Adding secondary ingredients to each of these will form different potions, and trying different combinations here will let you create the whole range of potions on offer.

There are three tertiary ingredients that you can then add to these potions, if necessary. The first of these, redstone, will increase the duration of the potion you have brewed, lengthening the time it affects you. Glowstone, on the other hand, will increase the potency of your potion, rendering it more effective upon use. Finally, a fermented spider eye will corrupt the effect of your potion – a useful tool if you want to make a Splash potion that you can throw at enemies to cause adverse effects. You can only apply one tertiary ingredient to a primary potion at any time, so choose carefully.

The essential potions to brew

1: Fire Resistance
Brew water with nether wart to form an Awkward potion, then with magma cream. It's useful if heading into The Nether – it'll give immunity to damage from fire, lava and Blaze attacks.

2: Healing
Create the Awkward potion again, but this time brew it with a glistening melon. Drinking the basic Healing Potion will restore two hearts instantly, and powering it up will double that.

3: Swiftness
If you're travelling a long way, or just need to get away from a group of enemies at speed, this potion will help. You can create it by brewing an Awkward potion with sugar.

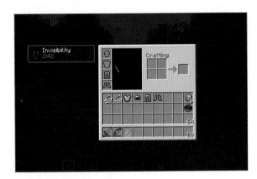

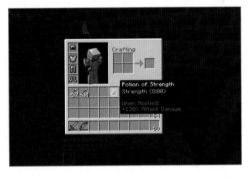

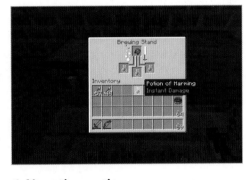

4: Invisibility
This potion makes you invisible to all creatures as long as you are wearing no armour. You can create it by adding a golden carrot to an Awkward potion, then adding fermented spider eye.

5: Strength or Regeneration
To create a Strength or Regeneration potion, add a ghast tear or blaze powder respectively to an Awkward potion. Strength adds extra damage to your attack; Regeneration restores health faster.

6: Negative potions
Adding a fermented spider eye to certain potions that have positive effects will create a potion with a negative effect. Drinking these yourself is foolish, but using them as Splash potions is a different story.

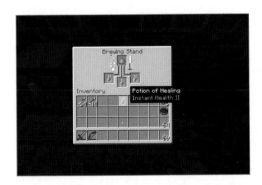

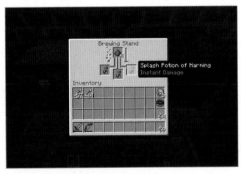

7: Extended potions
Adding redstone or glowstone to many primary potions will create Extended potions. These have effects that last longer or are more effective. It's worth saving up potions to add a little extra power.

8: Splash potions
You can add gunpowder to any brewed potion to make it into a Splash potion, which can be thrown like a grenade. This means negative potions can be used as offensive weapons against aggressive mobs.

9: Throw it!
Throw a Splash potion and you or any mobs within four squares will be affected. You can use them to heal friendly mobs – like wolves – or to kill others – like enemies – making them a valuable asset.

A guide to enchanting

Getting what you need to power up your weapons

When you have gathered enough diamond to create a set of tools and armour, you should start thinking about enchanting. With an enchanting table, you can spend the experience points you've earned from fighting enemies and mining on adding powerful extra skills and abilities to the items you've crafted. For example, if you want to give yourself a longer time when swimming underwater, you can enchant your helmet with a spell that will give you extra time when swimming. Alternatively, you can enchant your weapons with skills such as extra damage or a spell that will set enemies on fire when they're struck.

The effects you can add are really quite powerful and while it takes a while to built up the experience you need to gain the best enchantments, it's worth the wait. You'll get different results each time you try an enchantment, so if you don't like it the first time, try levelling up a little and trying again.

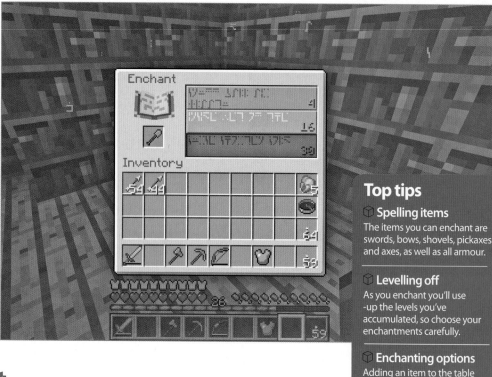

"You'll get different results each time you try an enchantment, so keep trying"

Top tips

Spelling items
The items you can enchant are swords, bows, shovels, pickaxes and axes, as well as all armour.

Levelling off
As you enchant you'll use -up the levels you've accumulated, so choose your enchantments carefully.

Enchanting options
Adding an item to the table will show you the options you have for levelling up the item.

Powered up
When you've enchanted an item and equip it, you will notice it glowing so you'll know it's special.

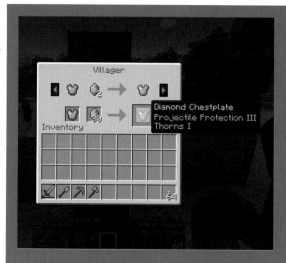

Trading with villagers

It's not what you know, it's who you know

When villages were first added to Minecraft, the only purpose they served was to add a little personality to the game world. Now, though, they can be quite useful. You can trade with any villager and depending on their profession, they will offer you different goods. If you find a librarian villager, you'll be able to purchase enchanted books that can be used on items. Alternatively, you can trade specific enchantments with a villager priest for a number of emeralds. You'll need to match what the villager wants precisely; right-click on a villager to see what they have to offer, and

place the requested items in the specific section. When the enchantment is complete, you can move the item back to your inventory.

There is no loss of experience associated with trading these items with priests, and there can be some really worthwhile trades if you can get hold of the items you need. Priests can enchant swords, pickaxes, axes and chest plates, and while there are a number of enchantment options for each one, each priest will only offer one enchantment option for each item. Try to find as many villages as possible, and try each villager when you do.

Key features

1: Books, books, books
You'll need plenty of books to create a powerful enchanting table. Add reeds near water to farm sugar cane, then place three in a horizontal row to create paper. Use these, with a piece of leather, to create a book. You'll need bookshelves.

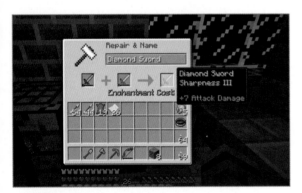

2: Repairing
If you have a damaged item that has been enchanted, create an anvil with iron blocks and ingots and you can repair it. Combining enchanted items can result in an equal or higher level of enchantment, although you'll lose one of the items.

3: Levelling up
You'll need to level up to get the most from your enchanting table. The higher your level, the better the enchantment levels available to you. You can level up by killing enemies, mining things like coal, or smelting items like iron ingots.

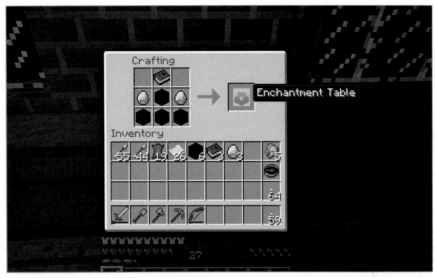

4: Building your enchanting table
Before you start enchanting, you'll need to craft an enchanting table. To create it, first gather some rare items, including a book, two diamonds and four blocks of obsidian. Once crafted and placed, the book on top will start spinning and when you place bookshelves around it, glyphs will start flying from the shelves into the book, indicating extra power.

"Glyphs will start flying from the shelves into the book"

5: The ultimate layout
When you place your enchanting table, you need to optimise the surroundings. Placing bookshelves around the table increases the available level of enchantments. There's a limit of 15 bookshelves that will increase the levels – adding more won't do anything. You can also only create a shelf two blocks high, and there needs to be a gap between the table and the bookshelves; this image shows a couple of good options for ultimate power.

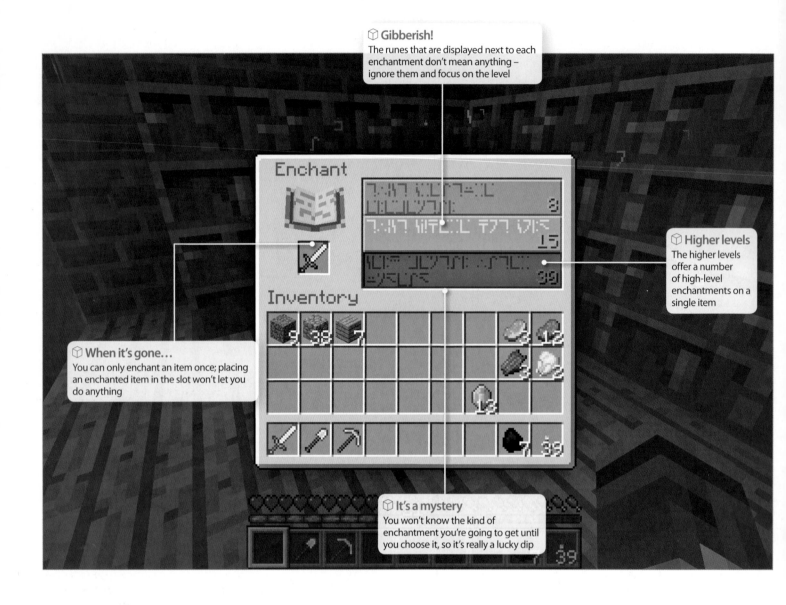

Gibberish!
The runes that are displayed next to each enchantment don't mean anything – ignore them and focus on the level

Enchant

Inventory

Higher levels
The higher levels offer a number of high-level enchantments on a single item

When it's gone…
You can only enchant an item once; placing an enchanted item in the slot won't let you do anything

It's a mystery
You won't know the kind of enchantment you're going to get until you choose it, so it's really a lucky dip

Learn to use enchantments

Discover how to enchant items, and the best options for each item

Now you've built your enchanting table, you can start thinking about which items you want to spend your hard-earned experience points on, and what kind of enchantments you want to get for each one. Only certain items can be enchanted, and while simply placing an item on an enchantment table and selecting the spell you want can gain most enchantments, others are only available via enchanting books. Whatever you choose to enchant, ensure you have enough experience to make it worthwhile; you can use a lot of experience on a single powerful enchantment or enchant a number of items with weaker enchantments, which cost less experience. Don't waste it.

Enchanted books can then be used on items with an anvil, or any other item to give them extra skills. Using enchanted books with an anvil will often result in enchantments that cost less than enchanting through the table, so it's worth giving this method a try.

Learn the basics of enchantments

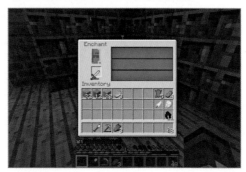

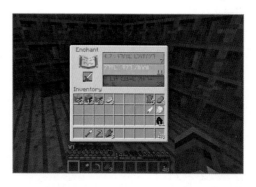

1: Level up!
Before you start enchanting, you'll need to gain some experience and level up. You can gain experience mining valuable blocks, smelting certain items and killing enemies. Start going out at night.

2: Add your items
When you're happy with your level, choose the item you want to enchant. You can add enchantments to armour, as well as swords, pickaxes, axes, spades and bows – just drop them in the slot.

3: Low level
If you only have a low level of experience, you'll see that there are only a limited number of enchantments available to you. If you want to get a higher level, you'll need to gather some more.

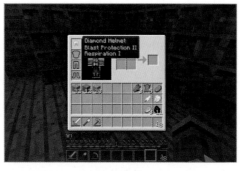

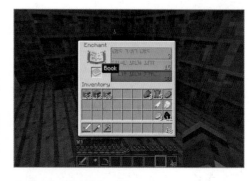

4: Life experience
With more experience, you'll be able to master higher-level enchantments, or a number of low-level enchantments on multiple objects. Think carefully about what you want each item to have.

5: Multiple enchantments
When you get to the higher levels of experience, you can get some very powerful enchantments. At around level 30, you can get multiple powerful enchantments on a single item with one spell.

6: Enchanted books
You can also enchant books: add a book to the enchanting table and choose the enchantment you want. These can then be used to enchant items (on an anvil) that couldn't normally be enchanted.

7: On the anvil
You can add an enchanted book to the anvil alongside another item to enchant it with the spell that the book holds. You'll need to build an anvil from iron blocks and ingots to do this, of course.

8: Repairing
Repairing items on the anvil will cost you some experience points, but the anvil allows you to combines two enchanted items and combine or enhance the enchantments as a result.

9: Make a trade
Another way to enchant is to trade with a village priest. You'll need emeralds to do it, but the result will be a randomly enchanted item that won't cost you any experience at all.

Sneaking
Hold the Shift key on your keyboard to sneak. You won't startle animals, and you won't fall off blocks

The Nether
Don't forget that travelling one block in the Nether is like travelling eight in the Overworld – a useful, if dangerous, passageway

Keeping animals close
You can keep tamed animals in pens, or tie them up with a lead attached to a single fence post

Potions
You can create a potion of Swiftness to increase your sprinting speed if you don't have animals or minecarts

Potion of Swiftness

Transportation options

Here are a few options for making travel faster and more comfortable

When you're working in a world that is – theoretically – completely infinite, getting hold of some good transport can make getting around much easier, and much faster. There are several options in this department, both naturally occurring and man-made. They all offer different speeds, and each one has advantages and disadvantages.

For example, building a boat is by far the fastest way to traverse the seas if you've spawned in an area surrounded by water and with few useful resources, but they're easily broken if you hit land too hard, meaning you'll probably need a few to ensure your trip will be completed successfully.

Minecarts are a great option, too; you can build powered rails that will shoot you down tracks at high speed, but to build these tracks you'll need a large amount of iron and a fair bit of redstone. These aren't items you come across regularly, so building longer tracks can be quite awkward.

Then, of course, there are animals to ride; pigs can be saddled, and while usually one will run randomly about as if you weren't even on its back, they can be controlled with a simple carrot. More on that shortly.

More recently, however, the developers of Minecraft have added a new form of transportation – horses. These animals can only be found in a

particular biome – the plains – so you might need to do some hunting, but when you find them you can tame one, add a saddle, and ride it to your heart's content. They offer the fastest transportation option available, so it's great to have a few tied up near your house. In addition, you can use these animals in battle, giving them armour to improve their ability to withstand damage and equipping a bow as you ride to shoot enemies.

In this tutorial we'll deal with the wealth of transportation options available, but you can turn the page for tips on building powered rail networks for the ultimate in hands-free travel.

Getting around in Minecraft

1: Find a saddle
To ride animals, you'll need a saddle. There isn't a crafting recipe to create a saddle, so you'll need to find one in a chest – they pop up in dungeons, temples and villages.

2: Ride that pig!
Right-click on a pig and you will add the saddle to it. Once it's saddled, right-click it again to get on. The pig will continue to behave normally without any player control in this state…

3: Carrot and stick
However, that all changes if you give the pig a little incentive. Add a carrot to a fishing rod in a diagonal formation and you'll create a carrot-on-a-stick that can be used to control the pig.

4: Taming horses
If you find a group of horses in a plains biome, you can start taming one. Right-click to get on a wild horse; you'll probably be thrown off several times, but eventually the horse will be tamed.

5: Going riding
Once the horse has been tamed, add a saddle to it. You can then ride it at any time by right-clicking to get on. You'll build up speed as you move, and automatically climb single blocks.

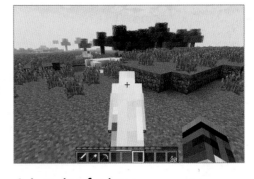

6: Jumping for joy
Horses can jump higher than normal animals, and they have a jump bar to show this. Hold the jump key to start charging your jump and let go at the high point to jump more than two blocks.

7: Player movements
Your character has several different movements, too. Double-tap forward and you'll sprint, which uses up food more quickly. Hold the Shift key to sneak, which helps when traversing thin bridges.

8: The seven seas
Build a boat from seven wooden planks and you can drop it in the sea. This allows you to traverse larger bodies of water much more quickly, although boats can be broken easily.

9: Flying by
In Creative mode, you can also double-tap the jump button to start flying. You will travel much more quickly when flying, and the only limits are the maximum and minimum heights of the world.

Getting started
Putting a switch next to a powered rail gives you a chance to get into your cart before it rolls away

On a slant
Starting a rail on a slant will ensure that your cart travels in the right direction

Powered rails
Create powered rails with redstone and lay them in intervals down the track to keep your cart moving

Obstacle course
If there is any object on the track and your cart runs into it, your cart will stop dead

Use rail networks for transport

Building rail networks makes crossing long distances effortless

One of the more advanced things you can do when thinking about getting around is building rail networks powered by redstone. These can be any length you want and as long as you ensure they are regularly powered, you can travel huge distances without any effort at all.

Rails, however, do take a while to create because each single block of rail requires six ingots of iron. To create longer networks you'll need to delve deep underground to mine all the materials you can, but once you've got it all you can zip across large distances in just a few seconds.

You'll also need to work with redstone to create automatic rails; you can find out more about working with redstone in the next section, but for rail networks it can really be quite simple, as you'll find out in this tutorial. So, forget about the effort of walking to your nearest village and create a quick route straight to it.

Take to the rails

1: Mine your materials
You'll need to mine a number of valuable materials if you want to build rails. You'll need iron for standard rails, and redstone and gold for powered rails, so it's time to get digging.

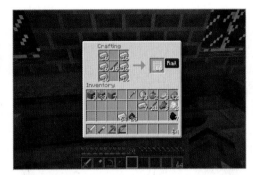

2: Building rails
You can form 16 rails with six iron ingots and a stick in this formation. You'll need a rail on every block that you want to travel across, so you'll need to craft a large number of them.

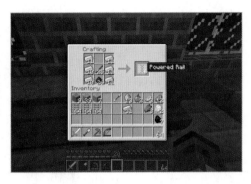

3: Powered rails
To create six powered rails you'll need two rows of three gold ingots, along with a piece of redstone and a stick. They are much more difficult to craft than standard rails, but you'll need fewer of them.

4: Laying it out
Lay out your track in as straight a line as possible; bends in the track will slow down your cart slightly, meaning you'll need to add powered rails more regularly, and therefore require more gold.

5: Power it up
To keep your cart moving, add powered rails regularly throughout the network. Each one will need to be powered, but that is as simple as placing a redstone torch next to the powered rail.

6: Maintain your speed
On a straight track on a level surface, you can place powered rails 28 blocks apart to keep your cart at maximum speed, although you will need to place them closer if there are bends or hills.

7: Starting blocks
Create a starting block by putting a powered rail on a hill pointing the way you want your cart to travel. Place a lever next to this and a cart on the rail won't move until you hit it.

8: Minecarts
You'll need minecarts to travel along the tracks. These require even more iron, but you can collect a minecart after using it by simply breaking it with a pickaxe or your fist.

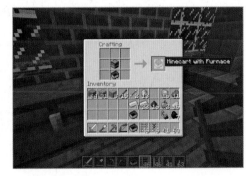

9: Special minecarts
Add items like chests, furnaces or TNT to an empty minecart to create a special minecart. Chests can transport goods, furnaces will power a cart like an engine, and TNT will create a moving bomb.

An overview of The End

A quick overview of what to expect from The End

When you've finally built up enough materials, armour, weapons, potions and enchantments and done everything else that the game has to offer, you can head to The End. This is meant to be the final port of call in the game and therefore you'll really need to have collected the best tools, gained the best enchantments and brewed many powerful potions if you want to go into The End properly prepared.

Getting there is easier said than done, too. You'll need a number of Ender eyes, along with blaze powder. You'll then need to find a Stronghold, where you will find the parts you need to open an End Portal, into which you'll need to place Ender eyes.

Once you're there, things don't get any easier – you'll need to avoid the Endermen that swarm around the main area, and do your best to take out the Ender crystals before taking on the Dragon itself. If you're ready for the challenge then read on…

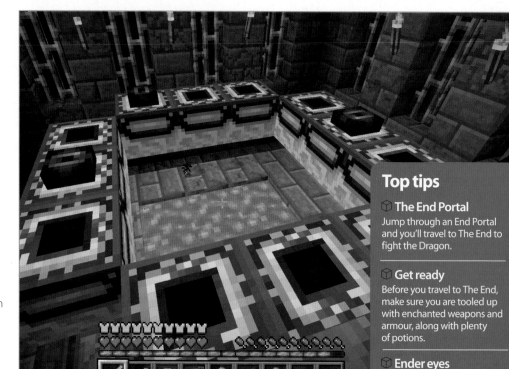

Top tips

The End Portal
Jump through an End Portal and you'll travel to The End to fight the Dragon.

Get ready
Before you travel to The End, make sure you are tooled up with enchanted weapons and armour, along with plenty of potions.

Ender eyes
You'll need to make a number of Ender eyes – some to find a Stronghold and the rest to activate the portal.

Stronghold
Strongholds are the only place you'll find an End Portal, so you'll need to find one to get to The End.

"You'll need to avoid the Endermen that swarm around the main area"

The Ender Dragon
Taking on the most dangerous beast in the game

There are a few important things to consider when fighting off the Ender Dragon. First of all, you'll need to make your way to the main island from the place you spawn. Be careful, though – the Dragon may attack while you're doing so and knock you into the abyss. Once on the island, you'll see several Endermen wandering around below.

The Dragon uses a number of attacks, swooping low to get close to you. The impact of the Dragon and its wings will cause great damage to you and knock you back some distance. Because of this, ranged weapons are your best chance for survival, although melee weapons will deal more damage.

The Dragon is immune to fire, so lava will do no damage, but surprisingly snowballs will deal damage and stun the dragon for a moment. Because of this, Snow Golems are a good idea, as are Iron Golems, which can combat any Endermen that you accidentally look at.

Attacking the Dragon immediately isn't the best idea – you need to take out the towers around the island before you battle the main beast. There are more tips on page 120, so head there for more information.

Key features

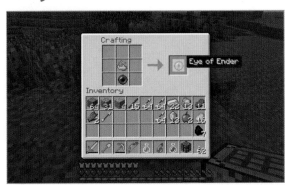

1: Ender eyes

Ender eyes are formed from an Ender pearl and blaze powder, and you'll need several in order to activate the End Portal. This will take some time, as Endermen can be difficult to find, awkward to kill and don't always drop a pearl when they die.

2: Tooling up

Before attempting to go into The End, you need to make sure you have all the tools and extra items you need. Enchanted armour and weapons are a good idea, and keeping a few potions with you will give you an advantage too.

3: The End Portal

You'll need to use an End Portal to get to The End. They will only be activated when you add 12 Ender eyes to the slots in the edges of the portal, so you'll need to kill plenty of Endermen and venture into The Nether for blaze powder.

4: Finding a Stronghold

In order to find a Stronghold you'll need to throw Ender eyes into the air. They travel in the direction of the nearest Stronghold and leave a trail of purple particles. Travel in the direction of the Ender eye and eventually you will find a Stronghold underground. It will likely contain a number of useful items, as well as several dangerous enemies.

"Travel in the direction of the Ender eye to find a Stronghold"

5: The Ender Dragon

The Ender Dragon is the final boss in the game. It's a huge beast that will fly around The End, swooping to attack you and recharging from the Ender crystals around the main area. It has a health bar that appears at the top of the screen, showing you how close you are to beating it. Hit it with projectiles to damage it; or strike at it with a melee weapon when it swoops low to attack, to do even more damage.

Preparing for The End

Gathering everything you need to fight the Ender Dragon

If you've never been to The End before, it's hard to know what you'll need to stand a chance against the Ender Dragon. Once you've reached the final realm, the only way out is death – killing yourself or being killed will spawn you back at your most recent bed without any of the items you took in. This means you'll want to make sure you are properly prepared with absolutely everything you need before venturing in. The last thing you want is to take a few items with weak enchantments and a single weapon, all of which took hours to collect, only to be killed and lose them all in a few seconds.

So, preparation is key; here we've shown the things you absolutely must have before you head into The End, but if you want to spend time creating extra potions, items and other weapons you can, to improve your chances further.

Get what you need

1: High-level enchantments
When enchanting items, ensure you don't scrimp on lower levels; level up to around 30 and use all your experience to gain powerful enchantments.

2: Weapons and armour
The key things to enchant are your armour for increased protection, your bow (you'll be using it a lot) and a sword to fight off any Endermen.

3: Arrows, arrows, arrows
You'll need a boatload of arrows; they're the easiest weapon to use when destroying Ender crystals and attacking the Dragon, so stock up on them.

4: Potions aplenty
Improve your chances by brewing potions. A Night Vision will make seeing the Dragon much easier, and Healing will give you a quick health boost.

5: Food for thought
Ensure you have plenty of food for the final battle – your health won't recharge unless your food bar is full, so make sure you stock up on cooked meats.

6: Golem allies
It's useful to build Iron and Snow Golems in The Nether, to help fight off the Dragon and Endermen. Take snow, iron and pumpkins to build them.

Find your way to The End

Making your way to the final boss is more challenging than you might think

Now that you've prepared yourself to fight the Ender Dragon, it's time to actually find it. The only way there is to find an End Portal, and these only appear in Strongholds underground. To find a Stronghold you'll need an Ender eye, formed from an Ender pearl and some blaze powder; throw the eye into the air and it will move in the direction of the nearest Stronghold. Once you've found it, you'll need to dig down and start exploring through its dark corridors, fighting off the enemies that have spawned until you find the Portal room. It's not over yet, though; to activate the Portal you'll need another 11 Ender eyes. This means a lot of Endermen hunting at night and a few trips to The Nether to collect blaze rods to break down into powder.

Find your way to The End

1: Ender pearls
To create your Ender pearl, you'll first need to find an Enderman. They spawn more rarely than other hostile mobs, so you'll need to search far and wide.

2: Blaze rod
You'll also need blaze powder, which can be obtained by breaking down a blaze rod. These are only found in The Nether, so you'll have to search for them.

3: Locate the Stronghold
Use the two materials to make an Ender pearl. Throw it in the air. It'll float away; follow it, pick it up and throw it again. Eventually you'll find the Stronghold.

4: Activate the Portal
You'll now need 11 more Ender pearls to activate the End Portal. Head back into The Nether and search for more Endermen to open your route to The End.

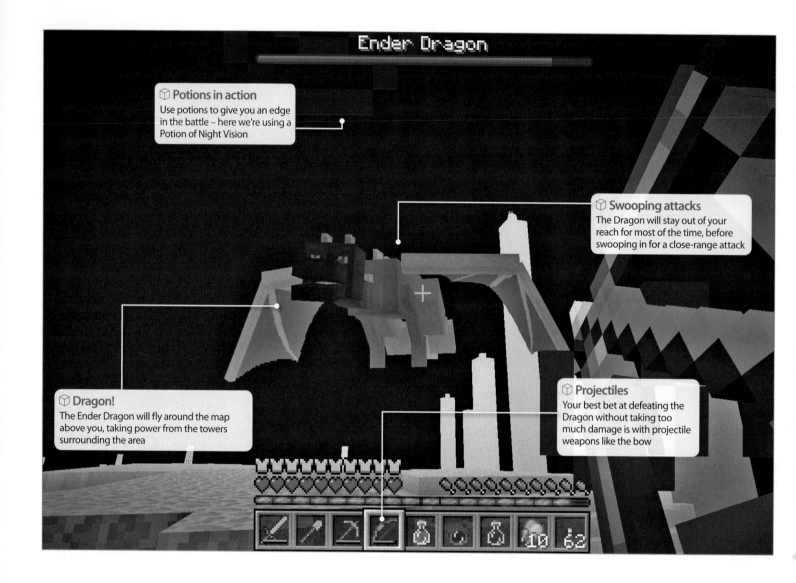

Potions in action
Use potions to give you an edge in the battle – here we're using a Potion of Night Vision

Swooping attacks
The Dragon will stay out of your reach for most of the time, before swooping in for a close-range attack

Dragon!
The Ender Dragon will fly around the map above you, taking power from the towers surrounding the area

Projectiles
Your best bet at defeating the Dragon without taking too much damage is with projectile weapons like the bow

Defeat the Ender Dragon

Top tips and techniques for taking down the flying beast known as the Ender Dragon

Now that you've got a Portal into The End, you can jump in. It's likely that you'll land on a platform of obsidian that is 4x4 blocks out over the abyss. Your first mission is to build a bridge across to the main area where the Dragon is flying; you can do this with any material, but watch out for the Dragon as it can still attack when you're moving across and knock you to your death.

You'll see a number of towers around the island, and it will be swarming with Endermen. Avoid looking directly at these Endermen if at all possible; you don't need another selection of dangerous foes to battle alongside the huge Dragon. If they do attack, concentrate your attacks on them until they're dead, then turn your attention back to the Dragon, as the Endermen pose a more immediate threat. As long as you're well prepared, though, you'll soon be collecting the Dragon Egg.

Beating the Dragon

1: Prioritise Ender crystals

First, turn your attention to the towers; on top are Ender crystals that allow the Dragon to recharge its energy. They can be destroyed with a single arrow, so concentrate on eradicating them all.

2: Improve your vision

It's very difficult to see the Ender Dragon in the dark; make sure you have several Potions of Night Vision, since they will make the Dragon stand out white in the sky.

3: Aim and fire

Use your bow again when the Dragon swoops in for an attack – it will be knocked back by your attack and as long as you hit it before it gets too close, it will fail to hit you.

4: Swordplay optional

Using a melee weapon like a sword will do a large amount of damage to the Dragon in a single attack, but you'll need to take a hit from the Dragon in order to damage it up close.

5: Healing and food

Take Potions of Healing and you can get an immediate boost to your health. You also need to make sure you keep eating food to help your health recharge automatically over time.

6: Beat the boss

The bar at the top of the screen shows how much life the Ender Dragon still has; when you've taken its final sliver of energy, it will rise into the air and explode in a ball of light.

7: Experiencing it

The Dragon scatters a huge amount of experience around when it dies; you can go from level one to level 76 in seconds, allowing you to gain more enchantments when you get back home.

8: The Dragon Egg

The Ender Dragon also leaves behind a Dragon Egg on a pedestal. This is directly above a Portal to take you back home, so build a platform around it to ensure neither the Egg or you fall in.

9: Pick it up

The Egg cannot simply be picked up – you'll need a piston to push it across a block in order to grab it. Activate the piston with a redstone torch, grab the Egg and head home – you're done!

Advanced Minecraft

"By modding Minecraft you can completely change the way the game looks, from your character to the world around you"

Introducing redstone

Discover the role redstone has to play in Minecraft

The true beauty of Minecraft is that it is as simple or as difficult as you, the gamer, want to make it. It is one of the many qualities that has made Minecraft into such a monumental hit. Fancy building a house and living out life on a farm? Go right ahead. Want to recreate the Sistine Chapel stone by stone and in scale? You can; it will take ages but if that's what you want to do then so be it.

For those of you out there who like a bit of complexity in your game, this guide is for you. Sooner or later you are going to find yourself discovering a strange mineral called redstone and, after trial and error, slowly discover its many uses. Over these pages we are going to delve into what redstone is, what you can create with it and why it is mostly used by the more experienced players out there, to construct elaborate circuits among other things. Hopefully after this guide you can count yourself among the redstone elite and know exactly what the difference between a dropper and a hopper is!

Top tips

Wire a circuit
Redstone wire connects circuits together. When the wire is live, it glows bright red.

Blocks
Redstone blocks are the basic – and main – source of power to make your circuits active or 'live'.

Powder or wire
To transmit power from a redstone block, you will need to use redstone powder or wire to create and complete the circuit.

It's electric!
The best way to think of redstone is that it is the Minecraft version of electricity and circuitry.

Making machines
Redstone is an essential tool to have when creating machinery, no matter how simple or complex the machines may be.

"Redstone is for those of you who like a little bit of complexity in your game"

What is redstone?

How important is this element of the game?

Redstone refers to the mineral collected after mining redstone ore, and it is mostly used within crafting and brewing. Redstone is mainly used to power automated and player-activated switches and panels within the world of Minecraft: think of it as a type of circuitry. This circuitry can be used to create anything from simple plate-activated doors or lights to complex elevator systems or truly functioning in-game computers that work perfectly.

While several in-game systems can perform information processing, only redstone was specifically added for its ability to manipulate information, by using redstone signals. Redstone has high reliability and switching speeds, which have helped it to easily overtake the other mechanical systems of Minecraft, just as electricity overtook various other alternatives to become the major power source for us.

Just as with everything else in Minecraft, once you understand how redstone operates and how to utilise it, you can delve as deep as you want. Beware though: the mechanics of redstone circuitry can be difficult to get your head around and some structures are so complex that you might never be able to create them perfectly. But persevere and you will be proud of what you are able to accomplish.

Key features

1: What is redstone used for?

It can be used to create many useful things: from pressure pads that open doors or turn on lights, to buttons that can power intricate minecart systems or even activate elevators. Redstone has so many different uses, many of which we will go into later.

2: Not a necessity

If you're just looking to make the usual creations and build whatever you fancy in the world, then you might find you never need to use redstone. If you want to delve into the complexities of the world, using redstone is a great way to do so.

3: Level of expertise

While creating a simple switch circuit that can open a door is useful and pretty simple, the more complex creations require so many different components that it can be easy to get confused or lost. It's up to you how you use redstone.

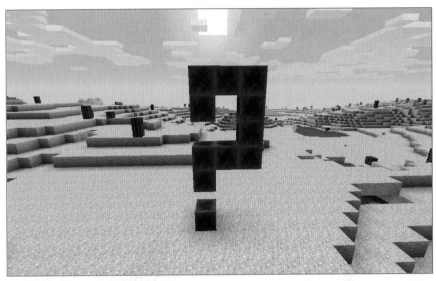

4: Redstone guides

In this section we'll tell you how to get the most out of using redstone and what exactly you can create with it. We will take you through the general guidelines of how redstone actually works, as well as listing the most useful redstone creations and how to put them together. Think of it as a how-to of redstone and how to get the most out of it.

"We will take you through how redstone actually works"

5: Creative or Survival mode?

Now this is totally up to you. Survival mode is the more difficult of the two choices as you have to gather the components while avoiding the dangers of the world. Creative mode gives you every item you can think of at your fingertips and a blank world to play about in. We would suggest you start with Creative mode, since getting used to redstone can be difficult and within Creative mode you can experiment to your heart's content.

The uses of redstone

Get started with redstone

If you are playing in Survival mode, redstone is mainly obtained by mining redstone ore. Killing witches and trading with priests can also gain you redstone, but it's less likely to drop so it's more difficult to collect this way.

While you can use redstone to brew useful potions, redstone is used primarily as a crafting ingredient for creating power sources and circuits that are useful in building simple-to-complex machinery. Understanding how to build redstone circuits and how they work will greatly increase what you can accomplish in Minecraft.

As with everything else in Minecraft, to create the entire components needed to get started, you will need a Crafting Table. The three main things that you need to create with the latter are redstone blocks, redstone torches and redstone repeaters. These creations are used in conjunction with redstone wire to power the various systems and mechanisms you can construct using redstone. Here we are going to go into more detail about what each of these creations are used for, as well as explaining how redstone wire works to connect power to your mechanisms. So let's get started!

"These creations are used in conjunction with redstone wire"

Top tips

Limits
Redstone wire cannot travel up vertical surfaces higher than one block.

Directions
Redstone wire can travel in any direction and power all adjacent blocks. It can also flow up any staircase.

Shades of red
Redstone wire is the thing you'll be using most. When powered, it is bright red; dark red when dormant.

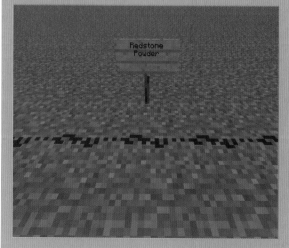

Redstone powder/wire

Essential to any redstone construct

Redstone wire is used to transfer power between power sources from block to block. It can be connected to other wires to form circuits, which are needed to activate or control your creations. To create redstone wire, all you need to do is place redstone on any surface and voila, you have the means to connect your mechanisms to a power source. When first placed, redstone wire will be coloured dark red, which means there is no power running through it; however, when connected to power sources, the wire will become live and appear bright

red and sparkling. Power will only travel through 15 blocks of wire before needing a new power source connected to it. The further away from its power source, the darker the wire will get.

You can tell how the wire is connected to other blocks by its shape. Placed on its own the wire looks like a dot, which can power any four adjacent blocks. When connected in all four directions it will form a cross, while connections on opposite sides of the wire will form a straight line. So it is easy to see what your power source is connected to.

Key features

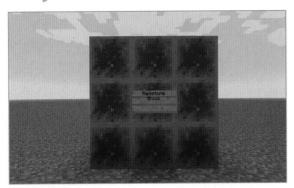

1: Redstone blocks
Redstone blocks are the major power source for mechanisms connected by redstone wire. They can power adjacent wire and also wire that is above or below the redstone block. These blocks provide constant power that can't be turned off.

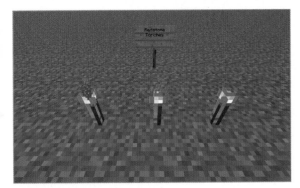

2: Redstone torches
Redstone torches have two uses: as a low-level emitting light source and, their main function, to provide a power source. They can power the length of 15 blocks in any direction and are useful in extending the power thorough longer circuits.

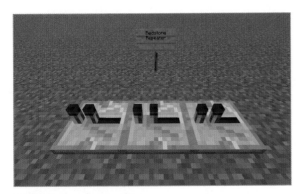

3: Redstone repeater
The repeater has a few functions. It can act as a diode (which can be used like a switch), a delayer (which delays the signal flowing through it), or as a repeater (which refreshes a redstone signal, allowing it to travel another 15 blocks).

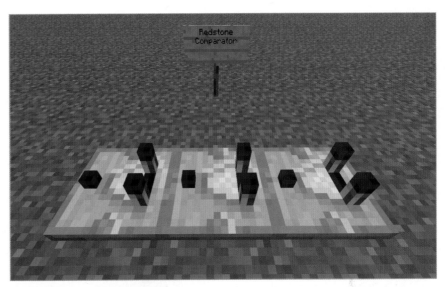

4: Redstone comparator
Comparators have two inputs – signal A from the back and signal B from the side – and have two different modes of operation. Subtraction mode will make the output equal to A minus B. Say signal A has a strength of ten and signal B one of eight; the output will be two. The comparison mode is useful for when you want signal A to override signal B.

"Comparators have two inputs and two different modes of operation"

5: Redstone lamps
A redstone lamp will emit a level 15 light which will keep enemy mobs away and stop them from spawning nearby. It is an opaque block, so if you power it directly it can cause adjacent mechanisms to activate as well, which can be used to your advantage. If the lamp has any redstone wire or switches adjacent to it – be they next to, underneath or on top of it – then they will be powered for one square respectively.

Build with redstone

Learn the components that go into creating redstone structures and mechanisms

Creating redstone circuits and structures is like anything else in Minecraft: it's as easy or as difficult as you choose to make it. To help understand how the circuits work, they can be broken down into three categories or components. These components are there to provide some purpose to your redstone circuits and help you to understand how they operate.

First there is the power component, which provides power to a circuit, such as a button or redstone torch.

Next is the transmission component, which passes power from one part of the circuit to another, mainly associated with redstone wire.

Finally, we have the mechanism component, which is the part of a circuit that affects the environment and will provide the final outcome, be it moving a door or turning on a light.

These three components are part of practically all redstone creations and knowing exactly what they do can help you understand the process and inner workings of your redstone mechanisms and structures. It is also essential knowledge if you wish to create the more complex and intricate circuits that are available to you in the game.

Top tips

⬡ The sky
The sky is literally the limit when it comes down to creating things in Minecraft using redstone.

⬡ Spawning enemies
When playing in Survival mode, watch out for spawning enemies that might kill you, since you'll then lose all your hard-earned items!

⬡ Digging deep
Redstone ore is found by digging deep into the ground. It is usually discovered in large open caverns.

"Circuits can be broken down into three categories"

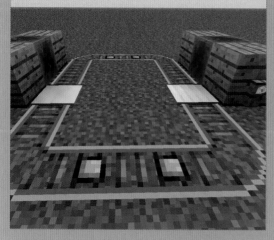

Other useful redstone creations
More redstone components available to you

⬡ While some creations are essential to put together circuits – like redstone wire, blocks and torches – there are loads of other mechanisms available to you that you can create for use with redstone that have more specific uses. Although the items on the next page can be pretty self-explanatory, they are included here because they can be extremely useful depending on what exactly you wish to build. From logic gates to the more advanced and complex redstone circuits, you will find a lot of the items here useful no matter what you plan to build or use them

with. Buttons, hooks and pressure plates are useful in most redstone mechanisms as they emit only a redstone signal to any structures or objects that they are connected to.

As with most things in Minecraft, the more in-depth you go into redstone structures, the more creations there will be available to you. No matter how complex or basic your circuits, just remember to make sure that all redstone components are 'attached' to other blocks in some way – otherwise they will eventually 'pop' (turn into items) if their support is removed.

Key features

1: Buttons

Buttons are used just like levers and need to be connected by redstone wire to the object receiving the charge (or next to it). They only stay activated for a short period. Stone buttons last for one second, while wooden ones stay on for 1.5.

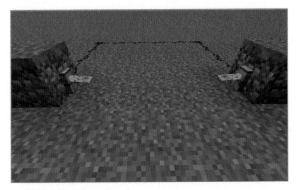

2: Tripwire hooks

Tripwire hooks need to be at opposite ends and connected by a tripwire or string. When something crosses the tripwire, the hooks emit a pulse of redstone. Hooks can be placed at a maximum 40 blocks apart and will lower once active.

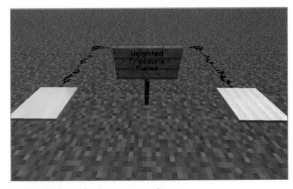

3: Weighted pressure plates

This variation of pressure plate emits a redstone current and come in two versions: a gold plate (light) emits a stronger current for every four blocks thrown on it; an iron plate (heavy) emits a stronger current for every item placed on it.

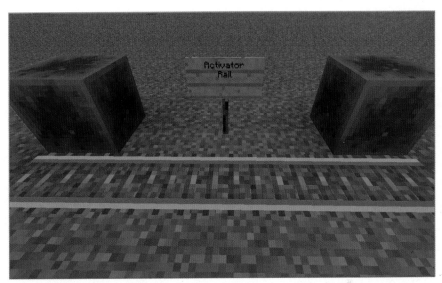

4: Activator rail

Activator rails act as normal rails do, but when given a redstone power source they turn on and activate any type of cart that passes over them. Although they can power any cart that passes, they do not accelerate or affect normal minecarts. Powered rails can set off TNT carts, which explode shortly after. The faster the minecart, the more powerful the explosion.

"Powered rails can set off TNT carts, which explode shortly after"

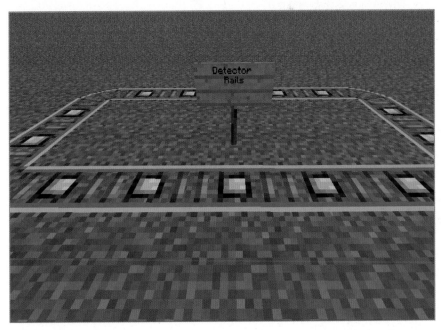

5: Detector rails

Unlike activator rails, which need a redstone power source to activate, detector rails actually generate a redstone signal when a minecart passes over them. This signal can be useful in powering blocks adjacent to the rail as well as acting like a pressure plate or switch. Because of this, detector rails are handy things to have and can be used for many different things, like powering longer rail networks or creating a one-way gate to a powered rail.

A guide to simple circuits

Now we have the basics down, let's take a look at some of the simple circuits you can build

Circuits are the basic structures needed to control redstone mechanisms. They can be created to operate in two ways: either on their own – such as in response to item drops or some kind of enemy activation (like an enemy tripping a trip wire or standing on a pressure plate) – or activated by the player, such as pressure plates, buttons or switches. Even though the terms 'redstone mechanisms' and 'redstone circuits' are used interchangeably, there is a distinction between the two. Circuits perform operations on signals and pulses, while a mechanism manipulates the environment, such as moving blocks or opening doors.

These can range from basic to complex. For example, even the opening of a door can feature either basic or more in-depth circuitry – it just depends on how you want to approach it. A basic circuit would use just a button to open a door, while more complex creations such as combination locks would have the same outcome but only open the door when a certain number of levers or buttons are switched on. The pass-lock doors are always useful for keeping your items safe while you're out.

Something to also keep in mind is the time it takes for circuits to switch on after you have activated the input. This is measured in ticks, which occur ten times per second. Redstone items such as torches and repeaters require at least one tick to change state. Obviously, the longer the circuit the more ticks or time needed for a signal to pass through it. Remember this if you wonder why your circuit isn't activating instantly or is taking a few seconds to actually propagate.

As mentioned earlier on, always remember that redstone requires the same three components to work: power, transmission and mechanisms. These three are fundamental to any redstone circuit and are handy things to remember when building your many different creations.

Building circuits

1: Door or fence switch

These very basic circuits just need a lever or button connected to a door or fence by powered redstone wire to work. They are perfect for farms and homes.

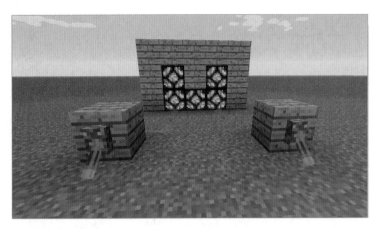

2: Light switch

Connect a button or lever to a redstone lamp with powered wire and you have a light circuit. Use lights/lamps as sections of your walls to light inside and out.

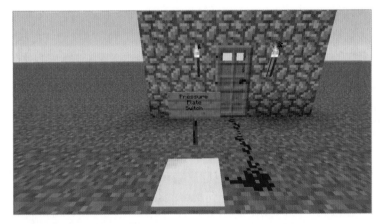

3: Pressure-plate switch

Stepping on a pressure plate connected to powered wire will activate whatever's on the other end, such as a door or trap. Great for opening a door hands-free.

4: Tripwire switch

Two tripwire hooks connected by string/wire can be used to set off a pulse of redstone when the wire is broken. Useful for powering connected traps.

5: Secret doorways and traps

Connecting a chest to a door/trapdoor via wire is useful as a secret lever to open hidden doors/traps so your items don't get stolen – especially in multiplayer!

6: Automatic lights

Powered redstone wire connected to a daylight sensor at one end and redstone lamps on the other can turn on your lights automatically when it gets dark.

Types of redstone circuits

We have broken the possible circuits down into six categories to help simplify the subject

While all circuits are made from three components (power, transmission and mechanism), there are certain categories that circuits can fall into depending on the desired outcome. Before we go into the different types of circuits, there are a few more things all you Minecraft players out there need to know about.

Some blocks are either powered or unpowered, with a powered block acting like it is electrified but not dangerous to touch. While there are blocks that will give off an indication that they are powered, like redstone wire, others give off no indication that they are switched on apart from what they do to

surrounding redstone components. Any power component will power a block strongly, while redstone wire will only weakly power the block it is connected to. You can tell if a block is strongly powered as it will activate nearby or adjacent redstone wire. When circuits are stable they produce an output, which is usually referred to as a signal. An ON signal means the circuit is powered, whereas an OFF signal means the circuit is unpowered. When you switch between ON and OFF, the signal that is sent out is called a pulse. Rather obviously, an ON pulse turns things on and an OFF switch does the opposite. Short pulses can cause problems with

some circuits because they cannot keep up with rapidly changing signals. So keep an eye on the way your circuit works signal-wise, as sometimes you may think it's not working when instead it's actually trying to keep up with the time delay.

Lastly we have the redstone update; this is when a change occurs within a redstone circuit which can produce a change in the surround blocks. These many changes can produce their own changes and so on and so on. These problems are common when trying to send redstone signals across long distances and discovering that the redstone update stops the signal from arriving.

Understand the types of circuits

1: Pulse circuit

Some circuits need specific pulses to work; others use the duration of a pulse to send specific info. Pulse circuits are needed to manage these circuits.

2: Transmission circuits

These send power signals from one place to another. Horizontal transmission is relatively simple, but a vertical transmission circuit is much more complex.

3: Clock circuits

These send out a loop of specific pulses over and over. They can be set to run indefinitely or for a set time, and can be stopped and restarted. Great for lights.

4: Logic circuits

These only send out a signal when certain input requirements are met. As the subject of logic gates is very extensive, we'll delve into them elsewhere.

5: Memory circuits

A memory circuit's output reflects the history of its inputs, not its current one. This allows it to remember what state it's meant to be in until told otherwise.

6: Multi-bit circuits

These treat their inputs as a single multi-bit value, performing an action on them all at once. Used to build complex mechanisms like clocks and basic computers.

Fix redstone circuit faults

When dealing with something as in-depth as redstone, and by extension Minecraft, you are bound to run into some complications. This section will help with any trouble you may find

There are many different types of problems you will encounter while building redstone circuits, so remember these handy tips. Here we'll go into the problems you may encounter along the way, as well as how to refine and expand upon circuits that you've come to know how to create. Of course, you should only think about expansion once you are comfortable with how redstone circuits are made and have a basic knowledge of their inner workings.

Be wary of water or lava near your circuits: when washed over by liquids, some redstone components will turn back into items or be completely destroyed

when touched by lava. This can be annoying when trying to create a mechanism that actually utilises water and lava, such as a slaughterhouse or a way of farming materials for enemy mobs. One wrong move can mean disaster as your whole circuit will disappear into nothing and all your hard work will go down the drain. Worse still is working with lava, which cannot only destroy your creations but you as well – and upon death, you lose every single item.

It can be useful to know which set of blocks you want to use when making circuits. Common choices are cobblestone, stone brick and even wood.

Also, when deciding what to create – be they simple or complex constructions – there are a few pointers you should think about before you get building, such as will your circuit be player- or mob-controlled? What mechanisms will be affected by your circuit? How and where will it be controlled from and how does the signal get transmitted from the control to the mechanisms? These questions are extremely useful to keep in mind when constructing circuits and mechanisms, as they can help you to work out what may be going wrong if your structure isn't doing exactly what you want it to!

Troubleshooting redstone

1: Problem-solving tips
When you have constructed your circuit and it isn't working how you want it to, the next few questions may help you to find out where you're going wrong. Lastly we will look at refining your circuits.

2: Little or no power
Are you trying to use a weakly powered block? Throw a redstone repeater next to it to strengthen the signal being emitted from the problematic block, or replace that block with a block of redstone.

3: Nothing flowing through a block
Is it a non-opaque block? If so, try replacing it with an opaque block; or if you don't want to do that, you can always build around the non-opaque block. The choice is up to you!

4: Circuit not activating correctly?
Are all parts behaving the way they should? Maybe you have crossed redstone wires which are sending the wrong signal from one part of the circuit to another. This is a common problem with circuits.

5: Torch isn't providing power
If your redstone torch is seemingly not providing power then it is possibly burnt out. Update the torch with a new one to hopefully power your circuit once again or chuck in a repeater.

6: Switches indirectly powered?
If your switches or pistons are being incorrectly powered then check if any of the nearby parts are providing a redstone pulse causing the indirect power. Check block by block to be sure.

7: Crossed wires?
Are there parts of the circuit activating when they shouldn't? You probably crossed wires, meaning you have a signal activating the wrong part of the circuit. Check your circuitry is all connected correctly.

8: Refining your circuits
Once you have a working circuit, you can look to improve upon the design. Maybe you can make it faster by reducing the number of components a signal has to travel through in your circuit?

9: Last few bits
Can you make the circuit smaller, more robust and reliable or even just expand upon it and make it larger? Have a play around with the circuits and components to see what you can discover.

Use logic circuits and gates

We are going to take a look at all the different types of logic circuits, usually referred to as logic gates. There are many different types, some of which we will go into below

Basically, a logic gate is a simple circuit that will give out a set number of outputs. The number of outputs is determined by the pattern of inputs, which are also referred to as the 'rules' of the logic gate. Logic gates are used a lot when delving into the more complex side of redstone. For instance, when building a basic computer you'll need to use a lot of different logic gates to get your computer up and running. This is just one example of how useful logic gates are when they are combined. While there is no real need for a computer in the world of Minecraft, it is just a way to show what

is achievable when you put your mind to it and effectively use all the tools given to you.

Once again, like most things in Minecraft, there are many types of logic gates that you can create – with each design having its pros and cons, such as speed, power and size. Although there are many varied mechanisms and creations you can make, the two most common when referring to logic gates are the OR gate and the AND gate.

An OR gate's output activates when any of its inputs are on, while an AND gate produces a signal only when all of its inputs are activated. Below

are the other types of designs you can use when creating your own logic circuit; once again, each one has its advantages and disadvantages.

Many people give up trying to create logic circuits when all of their gates seem to fail time after time. Just remember that if things aren't working or doing exactly what you want them to, then you just need take a step back, take your time and look at the circuit from every angle. Just keep practising and practising until you know how to make the easiest of gates and then progress on to the next circuit type.

The types of gates

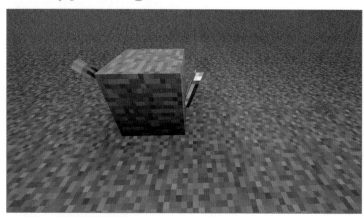

1: NOT gate or inverter
A NOT gate only activates when its inputs are switched off, not on. There are three types: subtraction, instant and torch. All three have their uses.

2: AND gate
An AND gate only activates when all its inputs are switched on. An example of an AND circuit is a door that needs both a lever and a button to open it.

3: OR gate
It only needs at least one of its inputs on to activate. Therefore OR gates can easily be combined to convert a huge number of inputs into just one output.

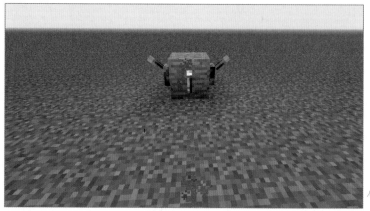

4: NOR gate
Its output is turned off when at least one of its inputs is switched on. You will probably use these most often when constructing your own logic gates.

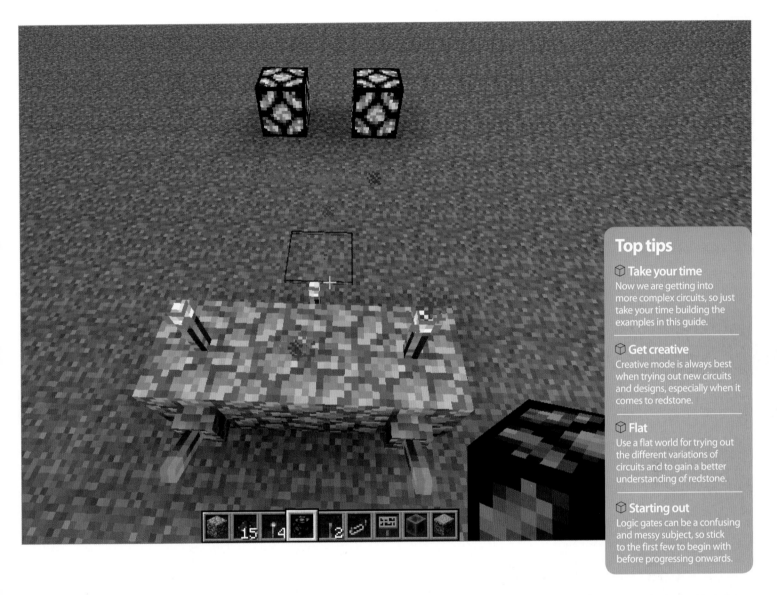

5: NAND gate
The opposite of an AND gate, it turns its outputs off only when every input is on. All logic gates in Minecraft can be made from a combination of NAND and NOR.

6: XOR gate
It activates when its inputs are different from one another (one on, one off). Add a lever to one to enable you to change the gate's output at the flick of a switch.

Understand clock circuits

Take a look at what clock circuits have to offer

Clock circuits, or generators, are circuits where the output is toggling constantly between on and off. Using only redstone torches and wire, it's entirely possible to create clocks as short as 4-clocks, but this is usually done by exploiting glitches. The name [number]-clock comes from half of the period length or time that they are on; using repeaters or pistons, you can easy construct anything down to a 1-clock, but these can be unreliable and unstable.

Speaking of 1-clocks, there is a type of circuit you can create that is called a rapid pulser. These send out rapid pulses like the 1-tick clock design, but their inconsistency causes the circuit to burn out the redstone torches for a few seconds. This is easy to spot, as all the other torches will blink. Obviously, this can be rectified by either replacing the burnt-out torch or adding more torches into the circuit.

Creating long clocks (anything more than a few ticks) can be more difficult, and adding repeaters can make the circuits unwieldy. Clocks without a toggle can often have one retrofitted, by wiring a lever or switch to the controlling block of an inverter. Whether the output will be stopped high or low depends on the clock and where in the loop you force it. Another option is to use lever-controlled pistons to open or close those loops.

Clock circuits can be a complicated beast of a subject at best; but, as we have stated earlier, just see how you get on with the easier structures and only advance to the more difficult when you feel ready. Torch loop clocks and repeater loops are the best ones to try out first, since they are the easiest to create without too much effort. It will also help you to get your mind around how clock circuits work and to see how they are different from the other circuits in Minecraft.

A closer look at clock circuits

1: Torch loop clock
The torch pulser has an odd number of inverters (NOT gates) in a loop. Using torches or repeaters comes in handy if you wish to extend the pulse.

2: Repeater clocks/loops
By using many redstone repeaters you can create a clock generator simplified into a single block, one redstone torch and connecting any number of repeaters.

3: Piston circuits or clocks
By using pistons you can create new types of clocks that have a changeable pulse delay. They are turned on and off by using a toggle input.

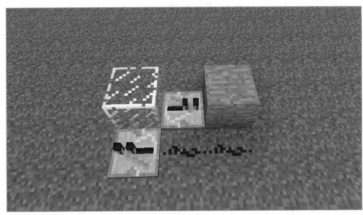

4: Comparator clocks or circuits
Subtraction clocks toggle on/off every tick and use a redstone comparator. Fader pulsers are useful for small clocks lasting only 1-15 seconds.

5: Hopper clocks or circuits
These can be made to last any number of ticks, to move things using the hopper loaded with items into and out of a number of containers.

6: Unique clocks or circuits
More exotic clock circuits include minecart clocks, cactus clocks (using cactus growth) and boat clocks (maybe with it lifted by water off a pressure plate).

Get to grips with pulse circuits

A deeper look into pulse circuits, their uses and the different types available to you

Like other redstone circuits, pulse circuits are hugely varied with many different purposes depending on the design. They all produce an outward pulse in response to its input being turned on or off, which are also referred to as rising and falling edges respectively. Some circuits can even use the duration of a pulse to send information back and forth between different circuits or mechanisms.

They come in three main variants. An edge detector sends out a pulse when it detects a change in its normal input; a pulse generator creates an output when its input is activated or switched on; and a monostable circuit sends out an output pulse of predetermined length when triggered. Another way to describe it is a circuit that turns itself off a set time after it has been activated. Some circuits are designed to lengthen or shorten pulses according to the maximum or minimum length.

We will go more in depth with these types of circuits below and why they can be useful to your mechanisms. One circuit we won't go into is the pulse delay design; this delays a pulse for a certain amount of time instead of just sending the pulse out as normal. It can be programmed to delay just the rising edge of a pulse, only the falling edge circuit or both at the same time. Lastly there is the oscilloscope, a sequence of redstone repeaters all set to a one-tick delay. Depending on how many light up, you can see how long the duration of a pulse is. Multiple oscilloscopes running together with many different circuits can help you compare the various delays of pulses being produced.

Again, like all things in Minecraft, we recommend playing around with pulse circuits to help you get an understanding of how they work, what they are useful for and where they should be implemented.

Understanding pulse circuits

1: Pulse generator
This only sends a pulse when its input changes. They are needed to clock flip-flops (inputs that toggle the output on/off) in circuits without a built-in trigger.

2: Variants in edge detectors
Rising edges activate when the input is on, while falling edges work with their input off. Dual edge detectors send a pulse when their input changes.

3: Inverted edge detectors
Basically the opposite of edge detectors. They are always on but output an off pulse (turns off then on again) when they detect an input change.

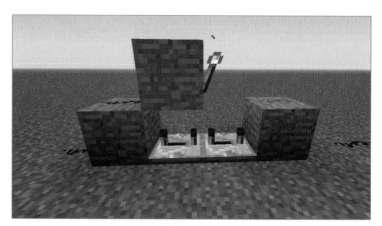

4: More on monostable circuits
These can be triggered by either a falling or rising edge or both at the same time. Useful for lengthening the duration of a redstone pulse in complex circuits.

5: Pulse limiter

This limits the length of a pulse. It can be useful to have in some circuits as to prevent multiple parts of the circuit being activated by the same pulse.

6: Pulse length detector

These can be useful to detect the length of a pulse generated by another circuit to check if it's longer or shorter than usual. They have many other uses, too.

Redstone minecart circuits

Take a look at some of the useful redstone creations available

Now that we have covered all of the versions of circuits you can create, it's time to go into what you can make by combining elements of the previous sections. Some are easier to create than others, from an airlock or a pass-lock door to more complex designs such as minecarts with multiple junctions or even working computers.

If you keep in mind everything we have covered in the previous sections, then just playing about with all the various circuitry will help give you a better understanding of how circuits work, from the basics to the more complex.

Certain redstone creations are more useful than others, whereas some are just so complex that they will need a huge amount of practice before you attempt to create them. The Morse code machine is a complex creation that springs to mind, the reason being that as of yet in Minecraft there is no specific use for creating a device to communicate; it is just an interesting experiment and shows off just how in-depth the subject of redstone can be.

"Certain redstone creations are more useful than others"

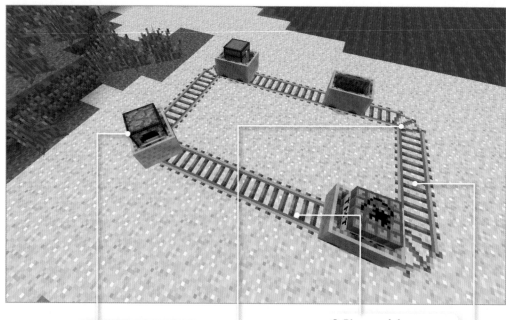

🔲 **Minecarts**
There are a few different types of minecarts available, from the regular empty ones to ones filled with TNT

🔲 **Using rails**
Remember that you need to use basic rails to create bends in the tracks as the special rails cannot do this

🔲 **Rises and drops**
Normal rails can be made into huge rises and drops which are particularly useful for building roller-coasters

🔲 **Going underground**
You can even use normal rails to go below ground level; these can be useful within underground mines

Minecart properties
All the variations you need to build a working minecart system

🔲 Out of all the things you can create with redstone in Minecraft, minecart systems are probably the most useful. From simple straight lines to complex rollercoasters, minecarts can be used in lots of situations. There are a number of different parts to the system. First up we have launchers; these are parts of the circuit where a rider can enter or exit a minecart. They generally use a button or a switch to launch the cart. Next we have rider detection; these are used to stop empty carts clogging up the rail lines – this is done by detecting whether a player is in the cart or not. Boosters are used to prevent minecarts from slowing down or stopping on a track; they are basically a method of keeping the carts going no matter what. Finally we have junctions, which are a fork in the track where the rider can select their preferred destination; these are useful for creating complex minecart systems which go anywhere at the press of a switch.

In this section we will go into how these work and how to create the easiest versions of the above points so you can mess about with what minecarts have to offer.

Key features

1: Properties of minecarts

Minecarts move further with a player or enemy in them than when they are empty. Slopes, pushing and powered rails help provide useful momentum. Minecarts will slow down or stop when not properly boosted.

2: What are boosters?

As carts will eventually slow to a stop on a flat track, boosters are a useful was to keep them going. Boosters can help to effectively counter the forces of gravity and friction on the acceleration of the cart on flat and sloped surfaces.

3: Minecart launchers

The most basic launcher uses a button, redstone wire, some powered rails and a redstone torch. The button activates the powered rail and launches the cart away from the solid block behind it. Launchers are also referred to as stations or exits.

4: Rider detection

A basic way to create a rider detection circuit is to use a tripwire-based design. While it will detect a player easily, it won't detect enemies like pigs and spiders. An empty minecart won't trigger the wire and so will be sent back where it came from, whereas an occupied cart will send a short pulse and continue along the rest of the track.

"An empty minecart won't trigger the wire; an occupied one will"

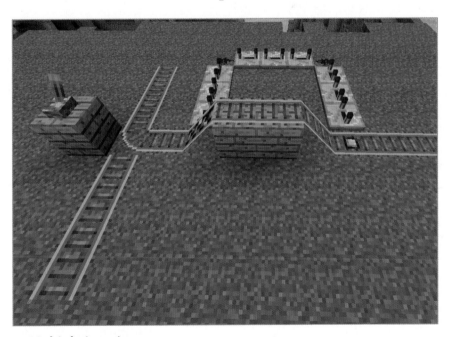

5: Multiple junctions

The easiest design for a junction uses a lever to switch the track and activate the corresponding powered rail – note that the lever should point to the selected destination. A junction that has many destinations can be created by expanding the junction to incorporate multiple directions and destinations. To create a junction with multiple destinations, the player needs to give the rider more time to select exactly where they want to go.

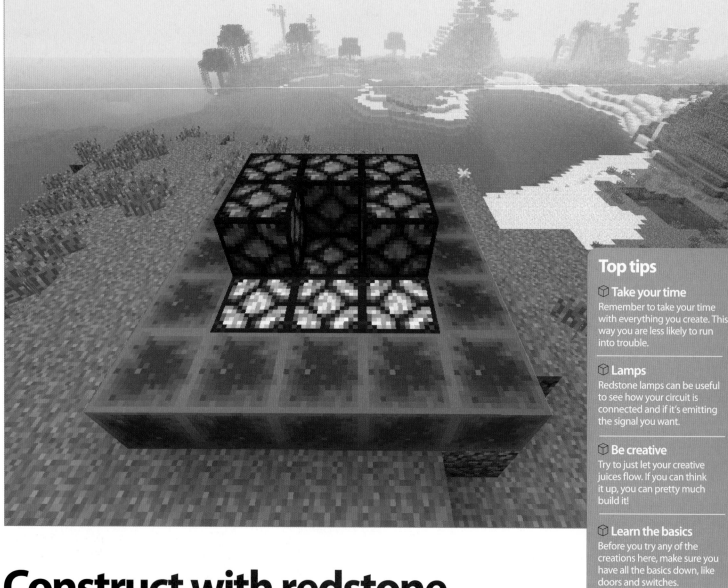

Construct with redstone

Now that we are into the complex stuff, we are going to go deeper into the more useful redstone mechanisms and circuits that you can build

While minecarts are possibly the most useful redstone creations, there are others available to you to try out as you please. TNT and mob traps are useful things to have for killing enemies and the local wildlife. As you may have guessed, these kinds of traps are most useful in Survival mode.

For the more adventurous and ambitious players out there, you can build an actual working computer or even a calculator that is never wrong. The computers alone have many layers, with some just consisting of redstone torches, repeater blocks and buttons. It's only the top layer that uses the

components combined with the redstone within to process arbitrary data. It is a true testament to the creators of Minecraft that redstone can be used in such a fantastic and complex manner.

Of course, these things require substantial items and an extraordinary amount of time to create, but if you can picture it, there is probably a way to build it. This is both the beauty of redstone, and the terror of it as well. It is no wonder a lot of Minecraft players out there have no idea about what to do exactly when it comes to redstone. Hopefully, after our extensive look at redstone, there will be more of you

out there that understand just how this beast of a material works.

One of the most fun things to make is a musical instrument, by combining redstone with note blocks. When powered by redstone, they play a musical note; the specific note can be changed by right-clicking on the note block, with each click increasing the pitch by a semitone. Minecraft players have been able to use these components to recreate a multitude of songs, from videogame soundtracks and tunes to complex classical music such as Beethoven's Ninth Symphony!

See what contraptions you can build

1: An hourly clock
An extension of a standard clock circuit, this indicates when an in-game hour has passed. Can be combined with note blocks so that it chimes on the hour.

2: Various types of traps
Most traps require redstone wire to power them. They range from covered trapdoors to flaming arrow dispensers, and can be as complex as you want.

3: Day/night detector
These can turn on lights indoors or outside your house to help prevent mobs from spawning. They also make a great decorative tile for roofs or tables.

4: Password-protected doors
Passwords are created by placing a redstone torch next to the corresponding levers and entering the numbers you want as your passcode.

5: Piston circuits
Using pistons lets you make circuits that are much smaller and/or faster than the redstone-only variety. Piston circuits don't burn out like redstone torches, either.

6: Redstone automated furnaces
Redstone wire can power a furnace that will cook any item, be it food or ore, and leave the finished product ready for collection from a connected chest or area.

Advanced redstone building

If you want to take things to the next level, here are some creations that can be useful and some that are just a bit of fun. It is handy to have a good range of knowledge regarding redstone construction

Redstone is a deep and extensive subject and to fully delve into all its secrets and various creations would take an age. There have been many players who have created wonders with complex circuitry and the like, but most players out there are happy enough with getting a door switch to activate correctly or a minecart ride to work without juddering to a sudden halt, and this is perfectly fine. You get as much out of redstone as you need. All we can say is do not be put off from trying new things; some of you out there may enjoy making circuits more than anything else, while others are

just glad to have some understanding of how redstone works.

Hopefully the overall guide we have given you will help you delve as deep into redstone as you want to go and will make your experience playing Minecraft that much more enjoyable. As they say, knowledge is power and nowhere else is it more evident than in this game.

Below are the last few examples that we think are great additions to your game. Sure, some of them are fun little things to have or use, but others may help you to create bigger and more in-depth

circuitry. For instance, by using a drawbridge you may feel the need to create a castle to accommodate and truly appreciate it. Maybe a castle with lights that activate when night-time arrives, a range of secret trapdoors and entrances and even a passcode lock to keep your valuables safe. All of these are redstone creations, which just goes to show that building one thing will usually inspire you to create something else entirely! This flexibility and drive to create whatever you wish is what makes most players jump into Minecraft head-first and use it as a canvas for their imagination.

Keep on building

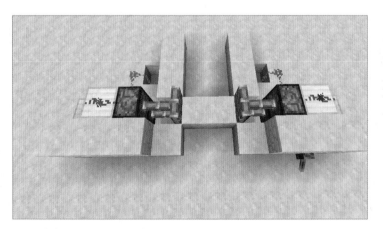

1: A redstone elevator
Combining redstone with pistons creates an elevator powerful enough to rocket you skyward super-fast! Careful on the way down, though, in Survival mode.

2: Animal slaughterhouse
By combining pistons, redstone repeaters and powder, you can create an animal slaughtering factory. This creation, once again, is more useful in Survival mode.

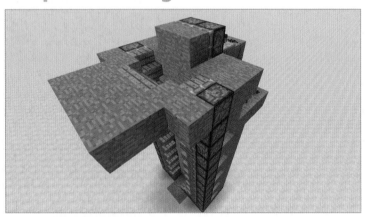

3: Hidden rooms and compartments
Using pistons and redstone, you can create a secret passage. Unlike normal hidden doors, piston doors can be activated from both sides.

4: A fully functional drawbridge
By using sticky pistons opposite one another, you can make them form a bridge at the flick of a switch. Deactivate it when full of enemies for a quick kill.

Top tips

⬡ **Imagination**
Imagination is the key. Just mess about with redstone in Creative mode to see what you can create.

⬡ **Test yourself**
Don't be afraid of making complex machinery. Remember that practice always makes perfect!

⬡ **Connections**
Keep an eye on all of the circuits and connections to make sure that they are all connected correctly.

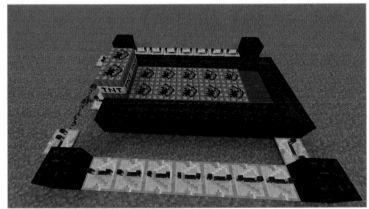

5: A TNT cannon
By using TNT and redstone, you can create a cannon that can fire anything from arrows and TNT to animals, enemies and yourself – vertically or horizontally!

6: A musical tune
As well as recreating popular songs and soundtracks, you can use note blocks and redstone to create your own tunes and sound effects.

Multiplayer, mods and more

Learn how to join multiplayer games, install mods and more

Minecraft is a game you can happily play on your own for hours, but it's all the better when you bring some friends with you. Whether it's working together to build a grand structure or even just to terrorise each other, as with most games, it's more fun with friends. Here we'll show you how to join other people's games on the PC and Xbox 360 versions of the game. We'll also be showing you how to change your skin so you can stand out among the other players of the Minecraft world.

We'll also cover mods – including our choice of the best mods out there – and how to install them so you can play them yourself. This isn't as complicated as you may think, so don't worry about pages upon pages of instructions. Mods can range from simple texture packs that change the look of the game's default blocks, to entire makeovers introducing new mechanics, items and gameplay styles.

Finally, we'll be going over how to earn some of the achievements in the game. There are a lot, but we'll focus on some that are harder to get.

Top tips

🗄 **Joining games**
Although the process differs on the PC and Xbox, it's simple on both counts. Play with friends for more laughs.

🗄 **Changing your skin**
This simple process will help you stand out in multiplayer. Why look like everyone else when you could be Superman?

🗄 **Get some mods**
Mods can overhaul the original game into something brand new, and breathe new life into Minecraft.

🗄 **Achieve things**
There are a mass of achievements for hunters out there. We'll help you get some of the more difficult ones.

"Mods can range from simple texture packs to entire makeovers"

Why play online?

All this fuss over multiplayer. Why should you do it?

🗄 Adding just one more person to a Minecraft world can make all the difference. Is a small house not good enough for you? Why don't you just build a castle? Well, that would take lots of time, surely. If you have a single friend playing with you it'll take half as long – that's simple logic. There are, however, other benefits.

Assuming your friends are nice, it's also a convenient way to gather materials you may not have. Giving a little to help them out should see you getting help in return, should you need something specific that they have.

This can cut down on the time spent looking for that precious piece of redstone you need, although your mileage may vary when asking for diamonds. Be prepared for a polite, or not-so-polite 'no' if you ask for that.

As with any other game, though, things are just more fun with friends. Of course, there's also the unintentional laughs that are guaranteed to come with Minecraft: the accidental falls when digging down, the sight of a friend in the distance running for their life from pursuing mobs, and did we mention the TNT traps you can set for fun?

Key features

1: Texture packs
These change the way Minecraft looks. There are also packs dedicated to making things look like a *Zelda* game, among the many other tributes out there. The best part is, they're simple to install and change.

2: A whole new game
Overhaul packs like Tekkit change the way Minecraft works, while generally retaining the feel and nature of the original game. They can simply add new items and recipes, or complex mechanics like electricity.

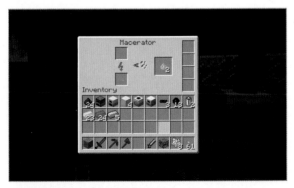

3: Expand your creations
While Minecraft allows the player to do a lot, mods can increase this. One pack may let you create a machine for breaking ore into dust which can then be smelted into more ingots, whereas another may expand the farming system.

4: Add more to Minecraft
The simplest reason for the existence of mods? They can add more of what you love. If you just like digging out ores and making things, mods exist that add more types of ore, and more weapons/armour you can make with them.

"Mods exist that add more types of ore and weapons/armour"

5: Back and forth
Given the way that mods work in Minecraft, a bonus is that you can generally switch between the modded game and the original game whenever you feel like it, should you decide that you want to play normally for a while. You can then switch back to the modded version easily when you decide you want to return to this, and vice versa. This means that you can try out new mods without any worries.

Change your skin on a PC

Learn how to change your skin so you'll stand out, or even create your own

It may be a simple thing, but changing your skin in Minecraft will really help you stand out in multiplayer games. It is easier to identify someone with a unique skin in a multiplayer game than squinting at the username floating above their head, after all.

While we will detail below how to download and change your skin the easy way, if you are a little more creative you can actually create your own. Thanks to websites like **minecraftskins.com**, this can be made relatively simple, with an easy-to-use editor that lets you create then upload your very own creation.

There are also countless skins on that site for you to download for your own use. They range from popular characters like Batman to the mad and wonderful, like a walking block of diamond ore.

Create a unique skin on PC

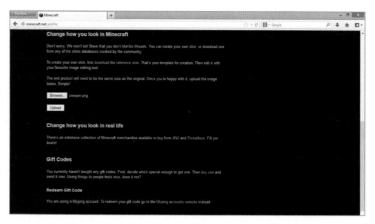

1: Download a skin
We're using **www.minecraftskins.net** for this. Simply find a skin you like the look of and download it to your PC somewhere you will remember, like your desktop.

2: Go to the official site
Next, log into your account on **www.minecraft.net**. Once logged in, click on the Profile option at the top of the page. This will lead to account options.

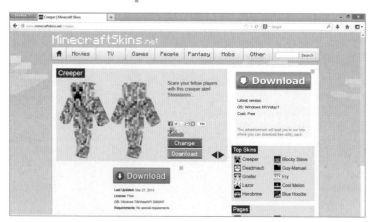

3: Upload your skin
On the Profile page, you'll see a section titled 'Change how you look in Minecraft'. Click on Browse and direct it to the skin you downloaded.

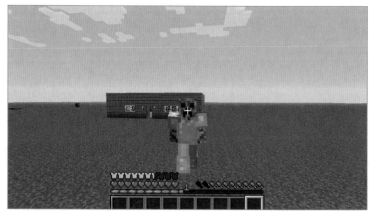

4: Finish the process
Next, press the Upload button. This will upload the skin and change your character. The next time you log into the game, you'll be using your new skin!

Download skin packs for Xbox

While a different process, you can also change the way you look on the Xbox

The Xbox version of Minecraft differs in a few ways from its big brother on the PC, and skins – and the way you change them – is one of these differences. Sadly, you can't create your own skins for the Xbox version, and so you are left to the mercy of the Xbox Live Marketplace.

To begin with, if you want to just use what is immediately available, there are eight skins by default. These range from the standard Minecraft Steve look to Tuxedo Steve, Scottish Steve and Tennis Steve, among others. To change between them, press the Start button and go to Help And Options, then Change Skin. From here you will be able to change between the available skins.

If you want more, you'll need to visit the Marketplace. We'll show you how to go about it here.

Download skin packs on Xbox

1: Go to the Marketplace
Go to the Game Marketplace under the 'Game' tab of the dashboard. Once there, do a search for Minecraft, which will lead you to the available goodies.

2: Select a skin pack
Skins on the Xbox come in packs, so your next job will be choosing the one you want to buy. Each contains a number of skins detailed in the description.

3: Purchase the pack
Next you'll have to go through the usual Marketplace buying process. Each skin pack costs 160 Microsoft Points, except the Festive Skin Pack, which is 80.

4: Get back in-game
Once you've bought your skin pack and it has downloaded, you can go back in-game. Press Start and change your skin – your new skins will be there.

Learn to mod Minecraft

Mods can add lots of new things for you, from simple tweaks to complete overhauls

Minecraft has a very active modding community. Fortunately for us, these talented people happily share their creations with the rest of the community, letting us all add new mechanics to the existing game.

Mods can range from simple texture packs that change the look of the game, to full-blown overhauls such as the popular Tekkit pack, which adds a host of machinery among other things. Generally these expansive mods will add an uncountable number of things to the game, but retain the original feel so it doesn't seem out of place.

Below we'll list our four favourite mods and packs currently available. And later on, we'll detail what they do and how to install them. Don't worry if you're not particularly tech-savvy: installing all of these mods is generally a pretty simple process.

Some of the best mods

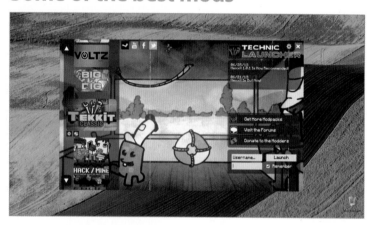

1: The Technic Launcher
This is one of the most popular launchers, and it makes things super-easy to get ready. It contains different mod packs in the launcher, such as Tekkit and Voltz.

2: Feed The Beast
Another launcher with various mod packs available, this one includes Feed The Beast itself and Ampz. All mods are downloaded through the launcher.

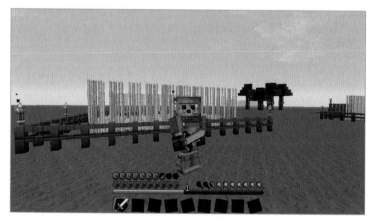

3: Texture packs
There are a huge number of texture packs available for Minecraft that can completely change the look of the world around you.

4: Download adventure maps
These are custom-made maps. While some can be infuriatingly bad, there are some real treasures out there from the highly inventive Minecraft community.

Follow adventure maps

Sometimes you may want a mission to do instead of open-ended freedom

Adventure maps are custom maps made by fellow players and are only available on the PC version. They typically follow a story, usually through signs or books, which the player can go along with.

A nice break from complete open freedom, adventure maps can contain tricky puzzles to solve, interesting stories to follow or jumping puzzles to infuriate you – there's generally something for everyone.

There are other types of custom maps, such as nothing but puzzles, or parkour-type maps, but adventure maps are the most common and that is also where you will find the most choice.

Once it has downloaded, place the map into the saves folder – C:\Users\Yourname\AppData\Roaming\.minecraft\saves. It will then appear in your saved games list the next time you launch the game.

Try these adventures

1: Star Wars

This has you completing three primary quests and three secondary, all *Star Wars* related. It can be found at **http://bit.ly/RNu77D**.

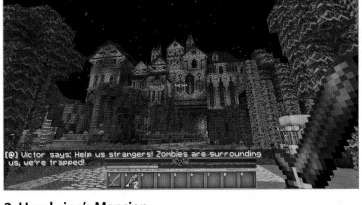

2: Herobrine's Mansion

Check out this map based on the old internet tale of Minecraft creator Notch's fictional dead brother, Herobrine. Get it from **http://bit.ly/SoiXa2**.

3: Minecraft Fallout

Taking one open world and throwing it into another, this is a clever map by Savethegnomes13. You can grab it yourself at **http://bit.ly/XqwN0l**.

4: World of Minecraft

A huge undertaking (and download), this gives you *World Of Warcraft*'s Azeroth to explore. Get it from **http://bit.ly/wqhsWa**.

Install texture packs

Installing a new texture pack has to be done manually. Here, we'll show you how

Texture packs change the way your game looks. These range from making the blocks in the game look more realistic, to looking cartoon-like, or even like *Star Wars*. Unfortunately installation is manual. Fortunately, it's very simple and will only take a minute to get set up.

Texture packs can be stored for later use, too. You can install as many as you like and switch them at will, even while you are playing. This is useful, as when downloading the pack may seem perfect for you but in practice you may decide you don't actually like the way it looks. All that would be required is a trip to the options menu to either restore the default textures, or select a different one you have downloaded.

Many websites exist for you to get new packs, and in this example we'll be using www.planetminecraft.com.

Change the way the game looks

1: Find a pack you like
Head over to www.planetminecraft.com/resources/texture_packs/ and find a pack you like. Press the 'Download Texture Pack' button to save.

2: Keep the file zipped
Out of habit, you may immediately unzip the texture pack you downloaded. It isn't necessary though, and in fact won't work if you do, so leave it as you got it.

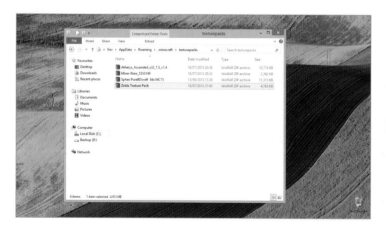

3: Move it to Minecraft's directory
It then has to be placed in Minecraft's 'texturepacks' directory. This is located at C:\Users\Yourname\AppData\Roaming\.minecraft\texturepacks by default.

4: Start the game
Once moved to the correct folder, you're done! Start the game and head to options, then 'Texture Packs'. Select your new one and you're all set.

The best texture packs

Change the way your world looks with these recommended texture packs

Texture packs are a means to changing Minecraft's default blocky look into something different. Sometimes they are used in custom maps to look exactly the way the creator wanted, sometimes you use one because you fancy something a little different.

Texture packs change not only the default blocks of the world, but the look of weapons, armour and items, and sometimes the default character skin (don't worry, if yours is a custom skin it won't change). Once you have them installed, you can switch between all your available texture packs at will through the options menu, meaning you can change how the entire game looks even as you're playing.

Below are four of our favourite texture packs that, while changing the look of the game, still feel perfectly in place in the Minecraft world.

The best packs for you

1: LB Photo Realism

This pack changes things entirely – it makes everything much more realistic, while still fitting with the nature of the game. Get it from **http://bit.ly/fgYWyq**.

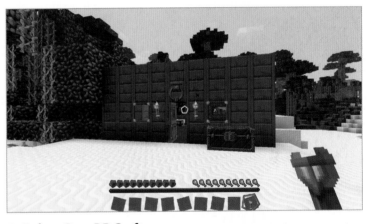

2: Sphax PureBDCraft

This popular texture pack gives things in Minecraft land a distinct cartoon-like vibe, where everything is vibrant and bright. Get it from **http://bit.ly/pcI53N**.

3: Mine Wars

A *Star Wars*-themed texture pack, which turns everything very sci-fi, lightsabers and all. If you want to be a blocky Jedi, you can get it from **http://bit.ly/ny9We2**.

4: Legend of Zelda

Another homage to a beloved franchise, this one makes the world of Minecraft resemble *Zelda* games, like *A Link to the Past*. Get it from **http://bit.ly/gzKvy5**.

Make chests!
If you hoarded in the normal game, you won't know what hit you. Make lots of chests

Have big bases
While it may look bare to begin, very soon your base will fill out with items, so make it large

Gather everything
On that note, gather everything you can store. It all has a use and it may be important later

Save your gems
You'll find rubies, sapphires and emeralds frequently. These can be used to create iron-quality tools and weapons

Explore the world of Tekkit

As it's one of the most popular modpacks out there, new or future Tekkit players may want a bit of an explanation as to why it has become so popular

Tekkit is very popular in the world of Minecraft. A simple YouTube search will return countless pages of videos and guides on it, and the popular gaming channel The Yogscast played a big part in advertising it to the masses. Put simply, it's Minecraft, but bigger and even more complicated. Take the base game, add more minerals, ores and recipes, then add machines, electricity, computers and even more advanced redstone and you'll get the idea.

To get it, you will need to download the Technic Launcher from here – **http://www.technicpack. net/download**. Once you have it, select Tekkit

Classic from the list of available packs and it will be downloaded and installed through the launcher for you. To run the game you must use the Technic Launcher instead of the normal Minecraft one.

Once you're in, things will seem pretty similar to begin, with one exception. You now have a fully functional mini-map. This isn't only useful for seeing where you are and what's around you, it can also track waypoints. Once you have built your first base you can set a waypoint there and as long as it's been activated, you'll always be able to find your way home.

The bigger differences come when you start to dig. Fairly quickly you'll come across a new ore-type: copper. You'll want to gather all of this. Any tin you see will also serve you well, so get that, too.

Above ground you may have also noticed (aside from one or two new block types) that there's a new kind of tree. These can be recognised by their tall, thin tips, and are called rubber trees. You'll notice the yellow blobs on the tree trunk; this is the resin, and to get it you'll need to make a treetap. Check out these pages for a recipe, as well as a few more which will hopefully get you off to a good start.

Start using Tekkit

1: Treetap
This is used to harvest the resin globs from rubber trees. See above for the recipe to make one, then once you have it, equip it and right click on the globs to use it.

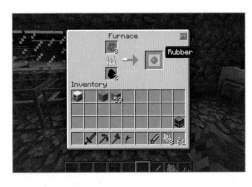

2: Burn the resin
Once you've harvested the sticky resin from the trees, you will want to put it in a furnace. Smelting it will turn it into rubber balls which is used in many of the new recipes.

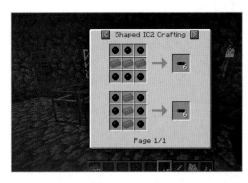

3: Use the index
Opening your inventory will show you every item in the game. To see what is needed to craft it, hover over the item and press 'R'. This will help you get accustomed to new items.

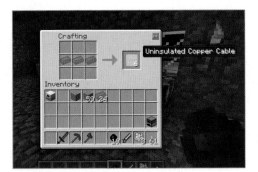

4: Make wires
That energy you have needs a way to power any machines you might make. To do this it will need wires, and this is where your rubber and copper comes in. Make some wires, as shown here.

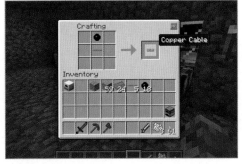

5: Insulate the wires
This isn't needed for basic energy but it's a very good habit to get into for later. Your new copper wires can be insulated with the rubber you gathered earlier. To insulate, use the recipe above.

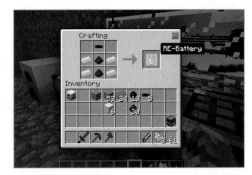

6: Make batteries
Batteries are used as an ingredient in a lot of recipes, so it's a good idea to know how to make them early. You'll need two redstone, one insulated copper wire and four tin ingots.

7: Get energy quickly
Almost everything you will make will require energy. A basic generator will cost you a machine block (eight refined iron, which is re-smelted iron ingots), a battery and a furnace. See the recipe here.

8: Making circuits
Circuits are also very important in many recipes. You will need six insulated copper wires, one piece of refined iron and two redstone to make just one electronic circuit. You'll be needing lots of these.

9: Your first machine
To get double the ingots for your ore, you are going to need a macerator. To make one you will need a machine block, three pieces of flint, an electronic circuit and two cobblestone blocks.

Join a multiplayer game on your PC

It's almost always better to play with friends.
We'll show you how to join them

Playing with friends is generally always the best way to play
Minecraft. But what good is that if you don't know how to play with
them? Here we'll show you exactly what steps you'll need to take to
join a friend's server so you can play together.

Aside from joining friends, you can also join random servers by
doing a quick Google search of Minecraft Servers. Just be sure to be
polite if you join someone else's server, don't join and then take their
items or break their structures, or you're likely to get banned.

Once a server has been added, it is saved in a list for easy future
access. It will show you how many players are online at that time,
and the maximum amount of players that can join, as well as your
signal strength.

Challenge your friends

1: Add a new server
When you select multiplayer, you'll see a host of options. To get started, select
the 'Add server' button, which gives you two new boxes.

2: Choose a name
This can be anything you like, it serves only to make a distinction among other
servers you may have saved and will be the name displayed on your server list.

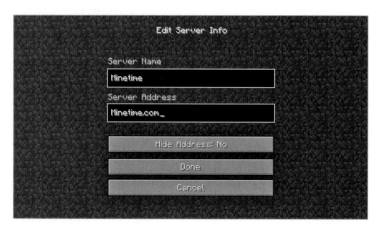

3: Get the IP/web address
If your friend is hosting, simply ask them for their IP address. If it is a server for a
website or community, find out their address if it's publicly available.

4: Save and go
Once you have entered a name and the server address, press the 'Done' button.
The server list will appear with your new server available to select.

Connect to a server on your Xbox

As with changing skins, the Xbox version has a different process to joining a server

With the lack of a keyboard and multiple options, joining a game on the Xbox 360 version of Minecraft is an even simpler process than it is on the PC. As a drawback, where you can join anyone with a publicly open game on the PC, with the Xbox you are restricted to those who are on your friends list.

    While this is inconvenient in limiting your server selection, it does stop random people coming into your game. The only way someone can get onto your server is if you invite them, and vice versa. Fortunately, there are plenty of community posts on the Minecraft forums with people offering their Gamer Tag and details of their own servers, should you be looking for a new one to join that suits your tastes.

Playing with friends

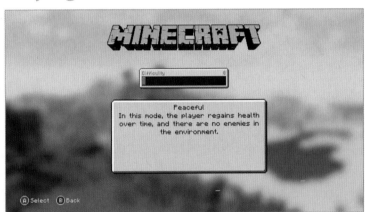

1: Add the host
If they aren't already there, you'll need to add the host of the server to your friends list. This can be done on your friends list by selecting 'Add Friend'.

2: Choose a friend
On the 'Load Game' screen, a list of your friends with open servers will appear, alongside your own saved worlds. From here choose which friend to join.

3: Joining private worlds
Even friends can keep their worlds private, to prevent anyone on their friends list jumping in. You can ask for an invite, which will let you join with their permission.

4: Play by the rules
A lot of players give a measure of trust by offering their Gamertag online for others. They don't have to, so be polite when joining and follow their rules.

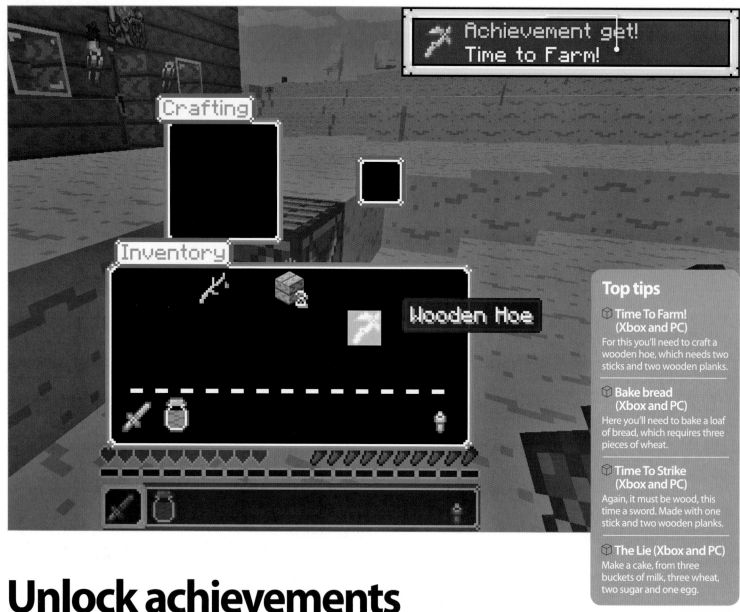

Unlock achievements

Both the PC and Xbox versions of Minecraft have their own achievements. Here we'll give you a little advice on how to unlock some of the more difficult ones on both platforms

If you are on a PC playing a new game, press 'E'! Congratulations! You unlocked an achievement! That one is called 'Taking Inventory', but unfortunately they're not all quite so easy to get. Some of the more difficult achievements can see you crafting things with rare materials or defeating a powerful enemy.

While most of the achievements are available on both systems, there are some that are exclusive to each – for example, the 'MOAR Tools!' achievement is Xbox 360 specific and requires you to make one of each kind of tool (a pick, a spade, a hoe and an axe), but the 'Return To Sender' achievement, where

you need to kill a Ghast in The Nether with its own fireball (done by hitting the fireballs with a sword to deflect them) is only available on the PC.

You will likely earn most of the easy ones as you play, but some will require more effort. Things like 'Monster Hunter' where you need only kill a single mob, or 'Cow Tipper' where you need to pick up leather from a fallen cow will come naturally; but achievements such as 'When Pigs Fly' will require you to find a dungeon before anything else, and find a saddle. Once you have the saddle you then need to find a pig to put it on, and proceed to ride

that pig off the edge of a high enough platform to hurt it. The PC version's achievement system works as a web, of sorts, where you'll on occasion need to complete a prerequisite achievement before you can get the next in the web. So in order to get the 'Time To Mine' achievement for creating a wooden pickaxe, you'll first need to unlock 'Benchmarking', which you get for creating a crafting table.

The Xbox 360 achievements have no prerequisites. They work and are displayed in the same way as all Xbox 360 games and can be unlocked in any order.

Top tips

Time To Farm! (Xbox and PC)
For this you'll need to craft a wooden hoe, which needs two sticks and two wooden planks.

Bake bread (Xbox and PC)
Here you'll need to bake a loaf of bread, which requires three pieces of wheat.

Time To Strike (Xbox and PC)
Again, it must be wood, this time a sword. Made with one stick and two wooden planks.

The Lie (Xbox and PC)
Make a cake, from three buckets of milk, three wheat, two sugar and one egg.

Uncover Minecraft achievements

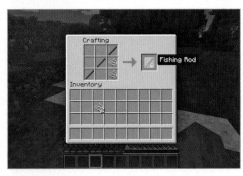

1: Delicious Fish (Xbox and PC)
For this achievement you will need to catch a fish. That in itself requires a fishing pole, made from three sticks and two string. Once you have a fish, cook it in a furnace.

2: Finding Diamonds! (PC only)
Finding diamonds may seem like an easy task, but it means digging very deep and even then, there's luck involved. You must find some and pick them up to unlock this achievement.

3: Dispense With This (Xbox only)
To unlock this you will need to build a dispenser. To do so, you will need a bow, a piece of redstone and seven cobblestone blocks, as shown in the image above.

4: Into The Nether (Xbox and PC)
Know as 'We Need To Go Deeper' on the PC. This requires you to make and enter a Nether Portal, made from 14 obsidian. You'll also need a flint and steel to activate it.

5: Into Fire (PC only)
This requires you to pick up a blaze rod, found in The Nether, only inside Nether fortresses. There you'll find the enemies Blazes. Once killed they have a chance to drop the rods.

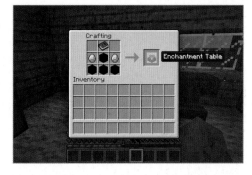

6: Become an Enchanter (PC only)
To get the 'Enchanter' achievement you will need to craft an enchanting table. This requires four obsidian blocks, two diamonds and a book. Not an easy task. The crafting recipe is shown above.

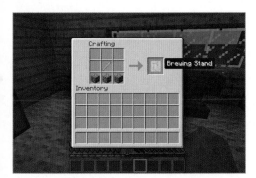

7: Local Brewery (PC only)
To unlock this achievement you will need to have a brewing stand in order to create a potion. The stand is made with one blaze rod and three pieces of cobblestone, as shown here.

8: The End? (PC only)
Here you will need to find a Stronghold deep underground. In it you will find an End Portal. Enter it, where you'll emerge in a different realm – The End. A foe awaits.

9: The End (PC only)
Simply exit The End. All you need do is defeat the Ender Dragon. Bring your best weapons, armour, potions, everything you have. Once the dragon's dead the portal appears and you can exit.

Crafting recipe reference guide

Whether it's a diamond pickaxe or a sticky piston, we've got the crafting recipes for every essential item you'll need

To make this book all the more complete – and to assist your experience with the sandbox craft-'em-up – we've bundled in all the craftable items you need so you can quickly and easily flick through and find the necessary ingredients and crafting patterns without having to leave the game. We've brought together a wealth of items you might need from the five main categories: tools, equipment, mechanisms, food and decoration. Tools are items that you'll need to use to craft in a game. Equipment are pieces of armour or weaponry that you might use to survive battles. Mechanisms are parts that you'll want to use in Redstone circuitry, and food is – well – self-explanatory. Decorations are items you can build to decorate your world, from paintings to beds.

Anvil Blocks of Iron + Iron Ingots

The anvil has multiple uses. To repair, place the item in the left slot and a material used to craft it in the second slot. To combine, place two items with the same enchantments in the first and second slots.

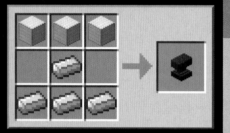

Armour (Leggings) Leather/Gold Ingots/Iron Ingots/ Diamonds

Armour is used to reduce damage taken from enemies. Leggings are the second strongest piece of armour and are equipped form the inventory screen. The better the materials used, the more durable the armour.

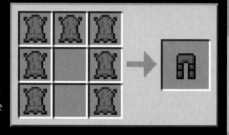

Armour (Chestplate) Leather/Gold Ingots/Iron Ingots/ Diamonds

A Chestplate is the strongest armour and can be equipped in the inventory screen. Using stronger materials will result in more durable armour.

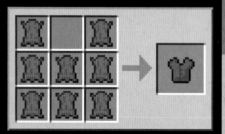

Armour (Helmet) Leather/Gold Ingots/Iron Ingots/ Diamonds

Helmets are the third strongest piece of armour and can be equipped in the inventory screen. Once again, using Gold Ingots, Iron Ingots or Diamonds will make the helmet stronger.

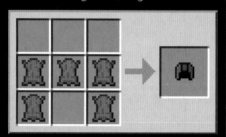

Armour (Boots) Leather/Gold Ingots/Iron Ingots/Diamonds

Boots provide the least amount of durability, but require fewer materials. The better the material, the more durable the armour. It is equipped in the inventory screen.

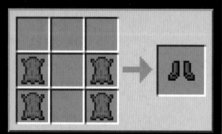

Axe Sticks + Wood Planks/Cobblestone/Iron Ingots/Diamonds

You'll need this to quickly chop wood of any kind. Initially you can craft the item from just wood, but this is the weakest of axes, meaning its durability is poor. Use Iron/Gold Ingots or Diamonds to make the best axe.

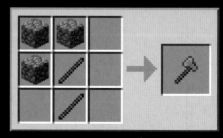

Beacon Nether Star + Glass + Obsidian

The Beacon is used to shine a beam into the sky, and to provide the player with a unique stats buff. It must be placed on top of a pyramid-like structure with a base of 3x3 crafted from either Gold, Iron, Emerald or Diamond Blocks.

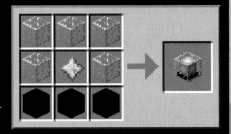

Bed Wool + Wool Planks (Any Type)

Beds are one of the more important decorative items since using them enables you to reset your spawn point (for if you die) and advance time during the night to morning.

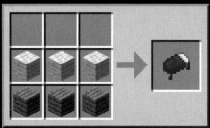

Blaze Powder Blaze Rod

Blaze Rods are dropped by Blazes after they are killed in The Nether. Blaze Powder crafts two at a time and is used in a handful of crafting recipes.

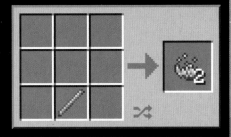

Boat Wood Planks

A boat can be used to travel across expanses of water. It is faster than swimming and doesn't sink, so a useful item as you look to explore further afield.

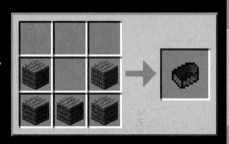

Bone Meal Bone

Bone Meal can be used as a fertiliser and can be used on a growing item for a chance to immediately finish the growing stage. It is also used in creating dyes.

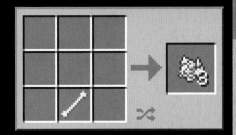

Book Paper + Leather

Books are a crafting material for a handful of useful items, such as Bookcases, Enchanting Tables and Book & Quill.

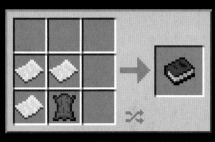

Bookshelf Wood Planks + Books

This block is most commonly used as decoration due to its appearance as a bookshelf, but is also necessary for enchanting.

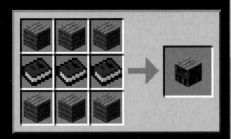

Bow Sticks + String

The bow is a ranged weapon used for attacking enemy creatures from a distance. It requires arrows as ammunition, which are automatically taken from your inventory when fired.

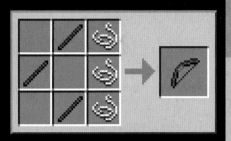

Bow (Arrows) Flint + Stick + Feather

Arrows are used as ammo for the bow. A single flint, stick and feather will craft four arrows for you to use in order to defend yourself.

Bowl Wood Planks

A bowl is used in cooking to store (and as part of the recipe for) Mushroom Soup. It can also be used to milk a Mooshroom.

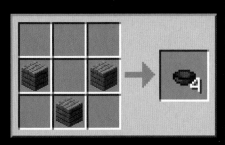

Reference guide

Bread Wheat

One of the simplest cooking recipes in Minecraft, Bread is a very basic food that restores 2.5 points of hunger.

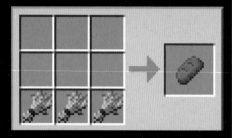

Bricks (Block) Bricks

This rather decorative block is most commonly used for buildings due to its red brick appearance. It is easily crafted from individual bricks.

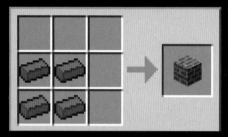

Button Wood Plank/Stone

The button is used to activate Redstone circuits by sending out a single Redstone signal. It stays active for one second before the signal is switched off.

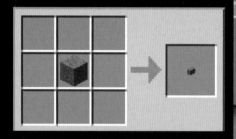

Carpet Wool

This is a decorative item used to apply a carpet to the floor. Each use of the recipe creates a total of three pieces of Carpet.

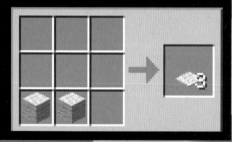

Cauldron Iron Ingots

Cauldrons are used in potion crafting. It can be filled with water from a bucket, which is then used to fill Glass Bottles necessary for potion brewing.

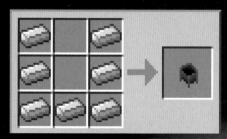

Brewing Stand Blaze Rod + Cobblestone

This is the tool with which you create potions of varying types. Right-click the Brewing Stand to open the Potion Brewing interface. Check the section on Potions for more detail.

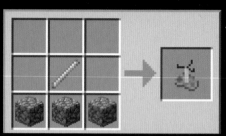

Bucket Iron Ingot

The bucket is a vital tool since it will allow you to carry water, lava or milk. Milk is necessary for making cakes and other food, while water and lava can be mixed to create obsidian blocks for Nether Portals.

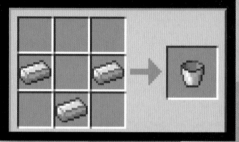

Cake Milk + Wheat + Egg + Sugar

A cake acts as a single block that can be placed in the world. Right-click to take a slice, restoring one point of hunger. A single cake has six servings.

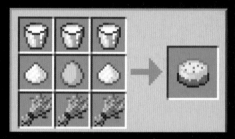

Carrot on a Stick Fishing Rod + Carrot

This is used to direct pigs while riding them (otherwise they'll go wherever they please). First you will need to craft a fishing rod, the recipe for which you can find elsewhere.

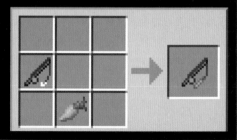

Chest Wood Planks

Chests let you store up to 27 items – of any type – to collect whenever you like. If you place a second chest next to another it will become a large chest. There needs to be room above a chest for it to successfully unlock.

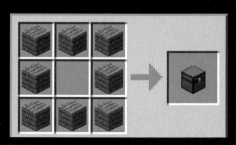

Chest (Ender) Obsidian + Eye Of Ender

The Ender chest works the same as a normal chest, except they share the same storage pool. All contents are shared between Ender chests, which means you can transport items around without having to carry them.

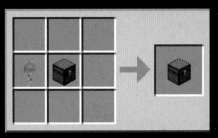

Chest (Trapped) Chest + Tripwire Hook

By opening this chest you activate a Redstone signal, which can be used to initiate attached systems. In the game this is most commonly used as a trap.

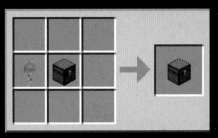

Clock Gold Ingots + Redstone

The clock rotates through images of the sun and the moon to tell you what time of day it is. This is useful when you are underground to know when to start heading back to the surface to avoid exiting a cave at night.

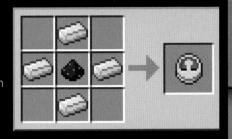

Compass Iron Ingots + Redstone

The compass will always point to the original spawn point – that is the centre of your world – and won't change even when you reset your spawn point with a bed. Use it for directions around the world.

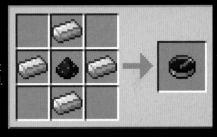

Cookie Wheat + Cocoa Beans

Eating a cookie restores a single point of hunger. A single recipe crafts a total of eight cookies, making it the most efficient cooking recipe.

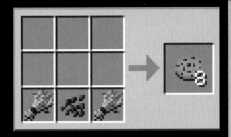

Clay Block Clay

This is the same block that you will destroy to find clay, but can be recrafted with four pieces of clay. It is a decorative building block or used as storage for clay.

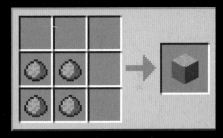

Crafting Table Wood Planks

The Crafting Table is one of the most important pieces of equipment you can craft in Minecraft, and will expand your crafting grid from the basic 2x2 in your inventory to 3x3. Without this the majority of crafting recipes cannot be accessed.

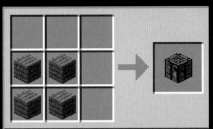

Daylight Sensor Glass + Nether Quartz + Wooden Slabs

As the name suggests, this is used to detect sunlight. When combined with various Redstone circuits it can be used to activate a system at a certain time of day since the Daylight Sensor measures the strength of lighting available.

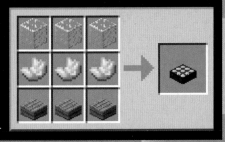

Dispenser Cobblestone + Redstone + Bow

A Dispenser can store nine items which are fired out of the block in a random order whenever it is right-clicked or activated with Redstone. Certain items can be shot out of the Dispenser to create a trap.

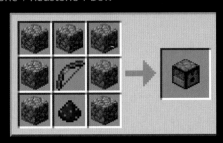

Door Wood Planks/Iron Ingots

Doors are used as entry points for your buildings and can prevent monsters from entering. Wooden doors can be opened by hand, but iron doors must be opened with a Redstone circuit.

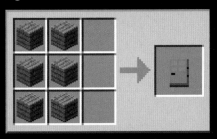

Reference guide

Dropper Cobblestone + Redstone

This works like the Dispenser except all items are dropped as though you have dropped them yourself. This means arrows, fire charges and other hostile items will not react like weapons, making it impossible to use as a trap.

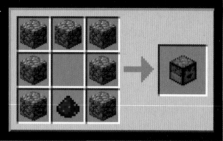

Dye (Light Grey 1) Ink Sac + Bone Meal

Light Grey Dye is used in colouring wool, leather or Hardened Clay Blocks. One use of this recipe crafts three pieces of dye.

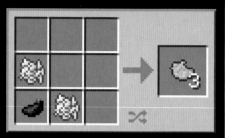

Dye (Light Grey 2) Grey Dye + Bone Meal

Combining Grey Dye with Bone Meal will make a lighter version of the dye. One use of this recipe will craft two pieces of dye.

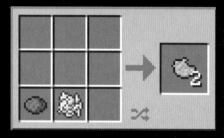

Dye (Grey) Ink Sac + Bone Meal

Grey Dye is the darkest of the grey dyes and can be used to colour wool, leather or Hardened Clay Blocks. One use of this recipe will craft two pieces of dye.

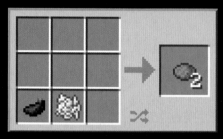

Dye (Rose Red) Rose

Rose Red Dye is used in colouring wool, leather or Hardened Clay Blocks. A single rose creates two pieces of dye.

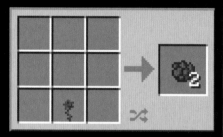

Dye (Orange) Rose Red Dye + Dandelion Yellow

Orange Dye is used in colouring wool, leather or Hardened Clay Blocks. One use of this recipe crafts two pieces of dye.

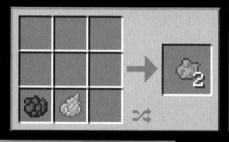

Dye (Dandelion Yellow) Dandelion

Dandelion Yellow Dye is used in colouring wool, leather or Hardened Clay Blocks. One Dandelion crafts two pieces of dye.

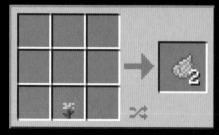

Dye (Lime) Cactus Green Dye + Bone Meal

Lime Dye is used in colouring wool, leather or Hardened Clay Blocks. It is the lightest of the two green dyes. One use of this recipe crafts two pieces of dye.

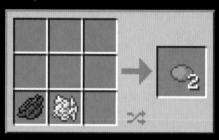

Dye (Cactus Green) Cactus

Cactus Green Dye is used in colouring wool, leather or Hardened Clay Blocks. It is the darkest of the two green dyes. It is created by placing the Cactus in a Furnace.

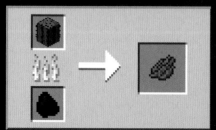

Dye (Light Blue) Lapis Lazuli + Bone Meal

Light Blue Dye is used in colouring wool, leather and Hardened Clay Blocks. One use of this recipe crafts two pieces of dye.

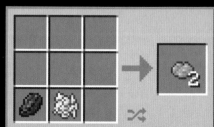

Dye (Cyan) Lapis Lazuli + Cactus Green Dye

Cyan Dye is used in colouring wool, leather and Hardened Clay Blocks. One use of this recipe crafts two pieces of dye.

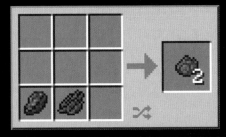

Dye (Purple) Lapis Lazuli + Rose Red

Purple Dye is used in colouring wool, leather and Hardened Clay Blocks. One use of this recipe crafts two pieces of dye. Purple Dye can be combined with Pink Dye to create Magenta Dye.

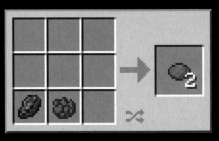

Dye (Magenta 1) Lapis Lazuli + Rose Red Dye + Bone Meal

Magenta Dye is used in colouring wool, leather and Hardened Clay Blocks. One use of this recipe crafts four pieces of dye.

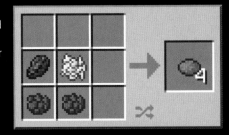

Dye (Magenta 2) Lapis Lazuli + Pink Dye + Rose Red Dye

Magenta Dye is used in colouring wool, leather and Hardened Clay Blocks. One use of this recipe crafts three pieces of dye.

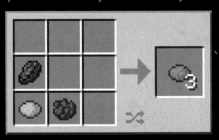

Dye (Pink) Rose Red + Bone Meal

Pink Dye is used in colouring wool, leather and Hardened Clay Blocks. One use of this recipe crafts two pieces of dye.

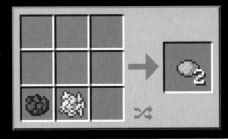

Dyed Wool Wool + Dye (Any Colour)

Dyed Wool is often used as a decorative construction material, usually for flooring of a building to represent carpeting. Dyed Wool cannot have its colour changed again.

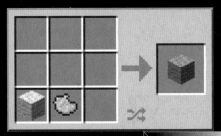

Enchantment Table Book + Diamonds + Obsidian

The Enchantment Table allows you to attach spells to tools, weapons and armour, and varies in strength and function. Surround an Enchantment Table by bookshelves for more powerful spells.

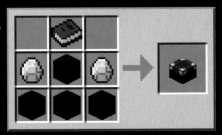

Eye Of Ender Ender Pearl + Blaze Powder

The Eye Of Ender is used to locate Strongholds and to repair an End Portal – the 'boss' section of Minecraft. Blaze Powder is crafted from Blaze Rods, while Ender Pearls are dropped by Endermen.

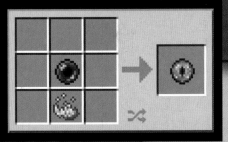

Fence Sticks

As you might expect this is used as a barrier and is primarily used to create pens for animals in farming. Counts as 1.5 blocks high for players and mobs, but one block high when placing blocks on top.

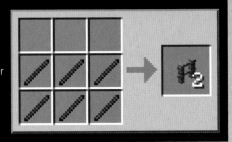

Fence (Gate) Sticks + Wood Planks

This is used as a door for fences and is useful for gaining access to animal pens during farming. It can be controlled manually or via Redstone circuits.

Reference guide

Fermented Spider Eye Spider Eye + Brown Mushroom + Sugar

Fermented Spider Eyes are used in potion brewing. Apart from the Potion Of Invisibility, Fermented Spider Eyes create Splash Potions with negative effects and should be used as weapons.

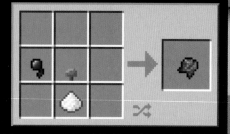

Fishing Rod Sticks + String

Cast the line of a fishing rod into a body of water and – when the hook moves – cast it back for a chance to catch fish. The fishing rod can also be used to pull monsters if you're careful enough.

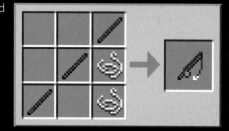

Flower Pot Bricks

As you might expect, Flower Pots are used to store plants. Saplings, mushrooms, cacti, ferns and dead bushes can be placed inside.

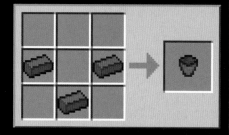

Glass Sand

This is a decorative block that – apart from some markings on the texture – are completely transparent. To make them, smelt sand in a Furnace.

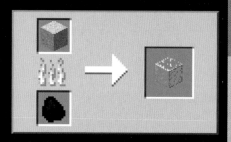

Glass Bottle Glass

These are used in potion crafting, and are used to store the drink. Three pieces of glass for one recipe crafts three Glass Bottles.

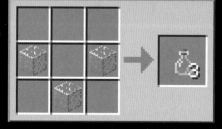

Fire Charge Blaze Powder + Coal/Charcoal + Gunpowder

Fire Charges can be used in dispensers to shoot fireballs, or used directly to set monsters or blocks on fire. Blaze Powder is crafting from items dropped by Blazes in the Nether, while Gunpowder is collected from slain Creepers.

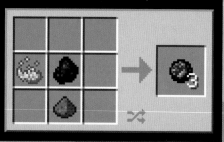

Flint And Steel Iron Ingot + Flint

This tool is used to create fire by clicking on flammable objects. There is a chance that flint will drop while digging gravel, regardless of whether you use your hands or a shovel.

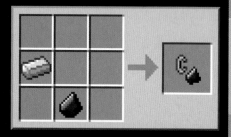

Furnace Cobblestone

Using a furnace will let you smelt ore into ingots or cook food to eat (cooked food fills more hunger than uncooked). Any form of wood can be used as fuel, but the easiest is coal. Each form of fuel has a set number of uses per piece.

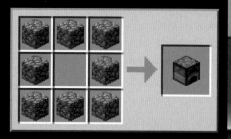

Glass (Pane) Glass

This works the same way as glass except that the pane stretches across the centre of a block rather than filling it. It is a decorative item used for windows.

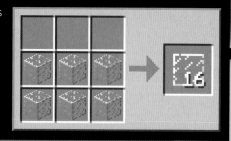

Glistering Melon Melon + Gold Nuggets

The Glistering Melon cannot be eaten, instead it is used as a component for health restoring potions in potion brewing.

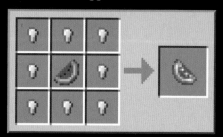

Golden Apple Apple + Gold Ingots

These special items restore two points of hunger as well as regenerate health for 30 seconds after eating. It can be eaten with a full hunger bar.

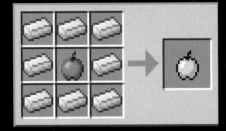

Golden Apple (Enchanted) Apple + Gold Blocks

This is much tougher to make but provides greater benefits than the basic Golden Apple. Alongside a stronger regeneration effect, Enchanted Golden Apples also provide resistance to Fire and Damage for five minutes.

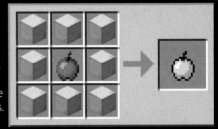

Golden Carrot Gold Nuggets + Carrot

Eating a Golden Carrot restores three points of hunger and greatly reduces your exhaustion (meaning you're able to take more actions before becoming hungry). It is also used in potions and to breed horses.

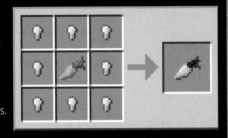

Gold Ingot Gold Nuggets

Gold Nuggets can be dropped by Pigmen of The Nether after you have killed them. Nine Gold Nuggets make a single Gold Ingot.

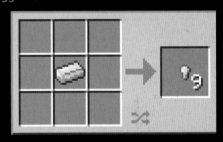

Gold Nuggets Gold Ingot

The opposite of forming a Gold Ingot, the reverse method can be used to create nine Gold Nuggets. These can be used as crafting materials.

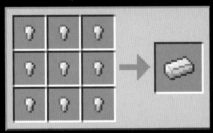

Glowstone Glowstone Dust

This decorative block can be used as lighting, and in fact is brighter than torches. You craft Glowstone from the dust retrieved after destroying Glowstone in The Nether.

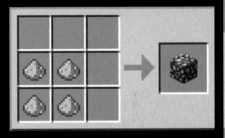

Hardened Clay Block Clay Block

Placing Clay Blocks in a Furnace bakes it to make Hardened Clay Blocks. This can be used as a construction material and can be dyed to alter its colour.

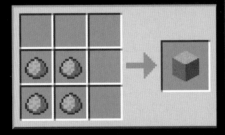

Hay Bale Wheat

While this can be used as a decorative block only, it is primarily used to feed horses. Right-click on a horse while holding the item to feed it.

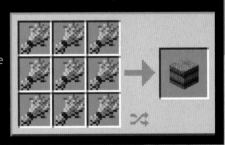

Hoe Sticks + Wood Planks/Cobblestone/Iron Ingots/Diamonds

This item is necessary if you want to start farming, since it is necessary to till the earth before planting seeds. The basic hoe can be crafted out of wood, but better materials such as Iron and Gold Ingots and Diamonds can make a stronger hoe.

Hopper Iron Ingots + Chest

Hoppers can be used to suck up items for storage and then used to transfer them into chests. It is a complex tool best used for more experienced Minecraft players.

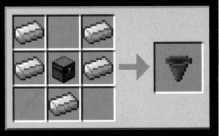

Reference guide

Item Frame Sticks + Leather

Item Frames act as display cases, and can be right-clicked to 'attach' an item of your choosing to it to display on the frame. Items like compasses, clocks and maps retain their functions within the frame.

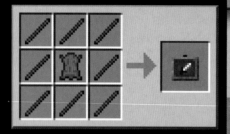

Iron Bars Iron Ingots

Used as a decorative item due to its appearance as a set of jail bars, this item is placed across the centre of a block rather than filling a full cube. One recipe crafts 16 Iron Bars.

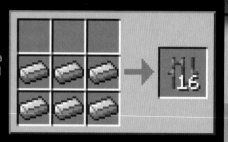

Jack 'o' Lantern Pumpkin + Torch

This is most commonly used as decoration but also has a brighter light source than torches. It melts snow and ice and can also be used underwater.

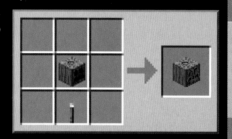

Jukebox Wood Planks + Diamond Gem

The Jukebox can be used to play rare Music Discs, which are either found in dungeon chests or dropped when a Skeleton indirectly kills a Creeper when attacking you.

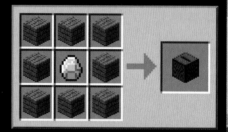

Ladders Sticks

Ladders are used to climb vertically and can be attached to almost any block. To climb, simply walk 'up' the ladder. One recipe crafts three ladders.

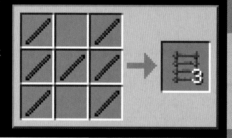

Leads Strings + Slimeball

This item can be used to tie up non-aggressive mobs (such as pigs and cows) to direct them around the world. You can use additional items while holding a tied mob, while right-clicking a fence will tie the lead to the fence.

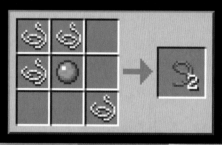

Lever Stick + Cobblestone

This is used to turn a Redstone signal on or off, activating or deactivating whatever it is connected to. This is necessary if you want to build circuits and the like.

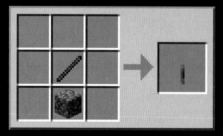

Magma Cream Slimeball + Blaze Powder

There is currently only one use for Magma Cream; it is used in a potion brewing recipe to craft a Potion Of Fire Resistance, which lets you swim in lava for a period of time.

Map Paper + Compass

When holding a map the terrain you explore will be displayed on the map, making it useful for navigation. Paper can be made from sugar reeds, and you can see how to craft a compass in this reference guide.

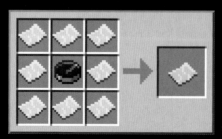

Melon Block Melon Slices

This can be used as a decorative block or as storage for your Melon, though it's worth noting that breaking a Melon Block will only return between three and seven of the nine slices it took to craft.

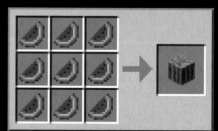

Melon Seeds Melon

Melon Seeds can be planted on farmland to grow additional Melons as requires. A single Melon will grow with each harvest.

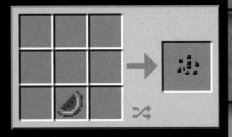

Minecart Iron Ingots

The Minecart is used in conjunction with rail systems to transport it (and any riders) along the rails.

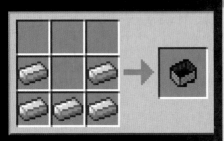

Minecart (with Chest) Minecart + Chest

This Minecart works the same as an ordinary Minecart except that it cannot be ridden. It can be accessed like a normal chest and is used to transport goods from one location to another.

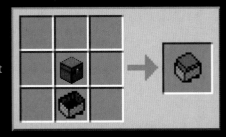

Minecart (with Furnace) Minecart + Furnace

This Minecart features a Furnace inside. It cannot be ridden like a regular Minecart, but can be powered with coal, wood or other fuel to push additional Minecarts along the rails.

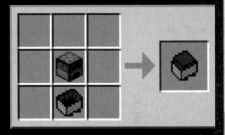

Minecart (with Hopper) Minecart + Hopper

This Minecart variant is used in conjunction with activator rails to absorb items lying on tracks and inside chests above them and then deposit them into another container elsewhere.

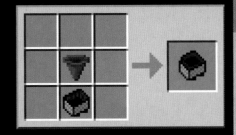

Minecart (with TNT) Minecart + TNT

This Minecart can be used in conjunction with rail systems and activator rails to create explosions. It is perfect for ambushes or traps on enemies and players (in multiplayer).

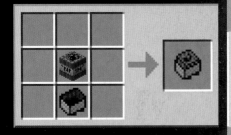

Mineral Blocks Any Ore x 9

These are solid blocks of ore. They can be used as opulent building materials or as compact storage of each ore. Redstone Blocks provide a Redstone signal to the adjacent blocks, and Coal Blocks are good forms of fuel in Furnaces.

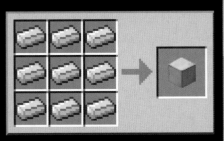

Mushroom Soup Red Mushroom + Brown Mushroom + Bowl

Eating a portion of Mushroom Soup restores a total of three points of hunger. Fortunately, the bowl is not consumed in the process.

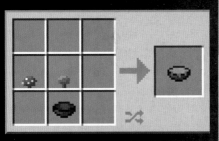

Nether Brick (Block) Nether Brick

This decorative construction block is found naturally inside The Nether at Nether Fortresses, but can be crafted from Nether Bricks (smelted from Netherrack).

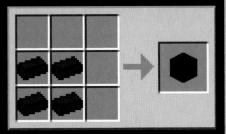

Note Block Wood Planks + Redstone

Plays a note when triggered (either by Redstone or a button). The pitch can be changed by right-clicking and the type of instrument depends on the type of block the Note Block is sitting on.

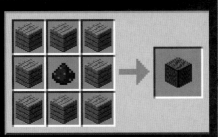

Painting Sticks + Wool (Any Colour)

A Painting is used as decoration and – when placed – will place a randomly chosen image from a bank of 26 available paintings of various sizes and design.

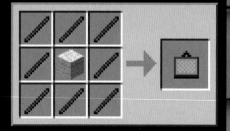

Paper Sugar Cane

Paper is used as a crafting material for maps and books. Sugar Cane is relatively easy to find, so you should be able to get your hands on plenty of paper when needed.

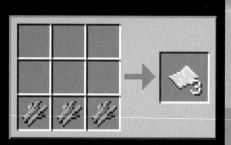

Pickaxe Sticks + Wood Planks/Cobblestone/Iron Ingots/Diamonds

Your basic mining item for collecting stone and ore. You can craft it from wood, but this is weak, meaning its durability and speed are poor. The better the material the better the pickaxe, with Iron, Gold and Diamond being the strongest.

Piston Cobblestone + Redstone + Wood Planks + Iron Ingot

A Piston can be activated with a button or lever or attached to a Redstone circuit. It is used to push blocks, items or mobs in a certain direction.

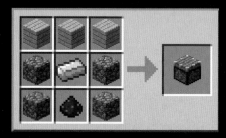

Pressure Plates Wood Planks/Stone

The Pressure Plate acts as a button and sends out a Redstone signal when it is activated. This can be placed on the ground and activated by a player or creature walking over it.

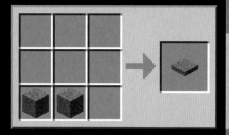

Pressure Plate (Weighted) Gold Ingots/Iron Ingots

This is the same as a normal Pressure Plate except it can't be activated by the player or creatures. Instead it provides varying Redstone signal strength depending on the number of blocks dropped onto the plate. Gold creates the lightest Pressure Plate.

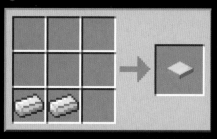

Pumpkin Pie Pumpkin + Sugar + Egg

Pumpkin Seeds are planted on farmland to grow additional Pumpkins. A single Pumpkin produces four seeds.

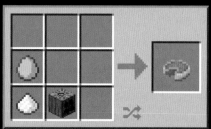

Pumpkin Seeds Pumpkin

Pumpkin Seeds are planted on farmland to grow additional Pumpkins. A single Pumpkin produces four seeds.

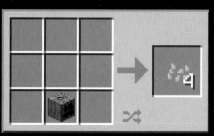

Quartz (Block) Nether Quartz

This block is a decorative block most commonly used in building construction. They cannot be broken back into individual Nether Quartz items.

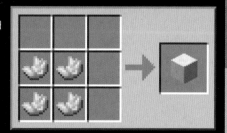

Quartz (Chiselled) Quartz Slabs

Chiselled Quartz is similar to Quartz except it has a pattern etched onto the side. It is more commonly used in building construction.

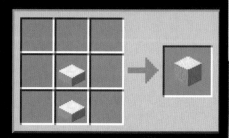

Quartz (Pillar) Quartz Blocks

A Quartz Pillar is similar to Quartz Blocks except it has a pattern etched onto the side to resemble a marble pillar. It is most commonly used as decoration.

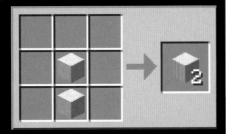

Rail (Activator) Iron Ingots + Redstone Torch + Sticks

The Activator Rail is used in conjunction with Minecart rail systems and is used to activate TNT Minecarts or Minecarts with Hoppers. The former initiates the TNT's timer while the latter enables or disables the Minecart's Hopper.

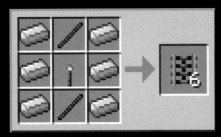

Rail (Powered) Stick + Gold Ingots + Redstone

The powered rail is used in conjunction with normal rails to speed up or brake a moving minecart. You can use Redstone circuits to toggle whether the rail is powered (speeds up) or not (brakes).

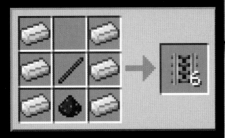

Redstone Repeater Stone + Redstone Torches + Redstone

This is used in conjunction with Redstone circuits to repeat a signal or to slow down a signal. Right-click to alter the speed of the signal response.

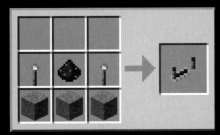

Sandstone Sand

This block can be found naturally in the world and most commonly used in construction. Unlike sand, it is not affected by gravity.

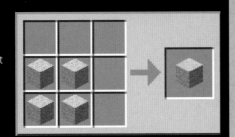

Rail Stick + Iron Ingots

This is a basic rail tile used to direct a Minecart. One stick and six Iron Ingots crafts 16 rail pieces – ideal for when you want to build a track for transportation.

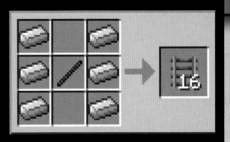

Rail (Detector) Stone Pressure Plate + Iron Ingots + Redstone

The detector rail piece is used in conjunction with normal rails. It functions the same as a pressure plate – therefore activating a Redstone signal – but can only be activated by a Minecart.

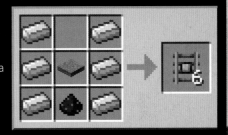

Redstone Lamp Redstone + Glowstone

Like standard Glowstone, this can be used to create an alternative, brighter light source than just torches. It can melt snow and ice and can be used underwater.

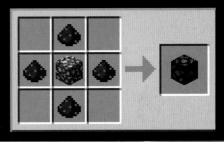

Redstone Comparator Redstone Torches + Nether Quartz + Stone

This is a more complex Redstone circuitry that is used to regulate a Redstone circuit system by only allowing a signal through once its strength reaches a specified strength. For experts only.

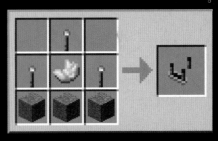

Sandstone (Smooth) Sandstone

Smooth Sandstone is similar to Sandstone except with a different texture. It is crafted with four blocks of Sandstone, instead of Sand.

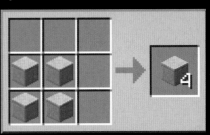

Sandstone (Chiselled) Sandstone Slab

This is similar to other types of Sandstone, except it has a pattern etched onto the side of the block. It is commonly used for construction and can be crafted with two Sandstone Slabs.

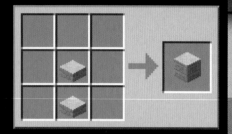

Shears Iron Ingots

Shears help you collect items that would be destroyed by hand. These are: dead bush, leaves, tall grass, vines and wool from sheep. Shears will destroy cobwebs, leaves and wool faster and can be used to collect tripwire.

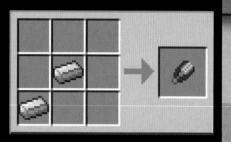

Shovel Sticks + Wood Planks/Cobblestone/Iron Ingots/Diamonds

The shovel is an optional tool that makes it quicker to dig up soil, sand and gravel. Initially you can craft the item from wood, but using Iron or Gold Ingots – or Diamonds – will make the shovel stronger and faster to use.

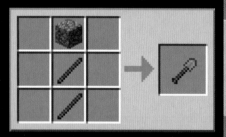

Sign Stick + Wood Planks

Signs are used as decoration, more specifically to name areas, buildings or even label chests with their contents. Right-click to change the message.

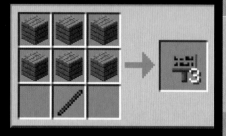

Snow Block Snowballs

This is a decorative block used as a building material or as storage for snowballs. It can also be used to craft Snow Golems, who are friendly to their creator but will throw snowballs at enemy mobs.

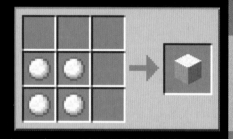

Sticks Wood Planks

Sticks are surprisingly important pieces of equipment for crafting and are used to create weapons, tools, torches, signs, ladders, fences and paintings. Using two pieces of Wood Plank will create four sticks.

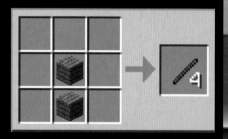

Stone Brick Stone

This is a decorative block most commonly used in building construction due to its appearance. Four pieces of Stone (smelted Cobblestone) makes four Stone Brick blocks.

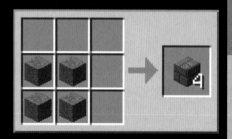

Stone Slabs Stone/Bricks/Nether Brick/Block of Quartz

Slabs are decorative blocks most commonly used for stairs. A slab is half the size of a normal block and can be walked onto without jumping. You could also use Cobblestone, Sandstone or Stone Bricks.

Stone Stairs Stone/Bricks/Nether Brick/Block of Quartz

Stairs are mainly used as decoration for your buildings to make navigation simpler. Six pieces of the same type of stone will craft four Stairs blocks. You could also use Cobblestone, Sandstone and Stone Bricks.

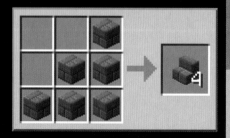

Stone Wall Cobblestone/Moss Stone

The Stone Wall is similar to a fence. It is intended as a short barrier, counts as 1.5 blocks higher for a player or creature but only one block high for block placement.

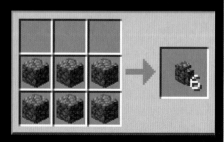

Sugar Sugar Cane

Sugar is used in cooking recipes such as Pumpkin Pie and Cake, as well as in potion crafting to create potions with speed effects.

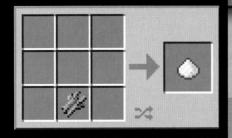

Swords Stick + Wooden Plank/Cobblestone/Iron Ingots/Diamonds

The sword is used as a melee weapon to attack enemy creatures. It deals more damage than by hand, while the better the material used the stronger the attack and the more durable the sword is.

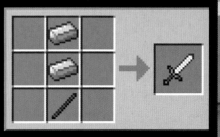

TNT Gunpowder + Sand

TNT is used to create large explosions that destroy the terrain around it. Useful for creating devastating traps or creating caverns. It can be set alight with a flint and steel, or activated with Redstone.

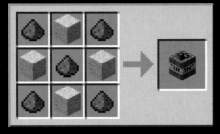

Torches Stick + Coal/Charcoal

This is your primary tool for lighting the underground caverns – and even lighting your home and surrounding environment. A single stick and piece of coal or charcoal will craft four torches.

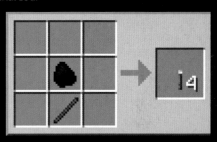

Trapdoors Wood Planks

Trapdoors are 1x1 doors that can be placed on the ground. They can be activated by Redstone signals. Six pieces of Wood Planks creates two Trapdoors.

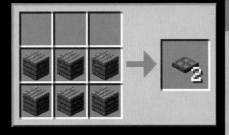

Tripwire Hook Iron Ingot + Stick + Wood Plank

Used to activate a Redstone signal whenever a player or monster steps on it. Used most commonly in traps. Some items – such as arrows – will not activate Tripwire Hooks.

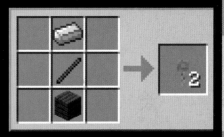

Wooden Planks Wood (Any Type)

Wood Planks are just another material used for crafting, but a regularly used one. It can be used for stairs, slabs and other decorative items. One piece of wood creates four Wood Planks.

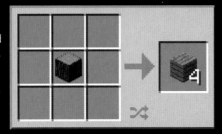

Wood Slabs Wood Planks

Slabs are a decorative block most commonly used for stairs. A slab is half the size of a normal block and can be walked onto instead of jumping. Three blocks of Wood Planks makes six Wood Slabs.

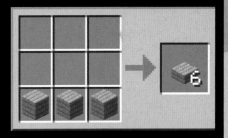

Wood Stairs Wood Planks (Any Type)

Stairs are most commonly used as decoration in your buildings to make navigation simpler. Six pieces of wood (of the same type) crafts four Stairs blocks.

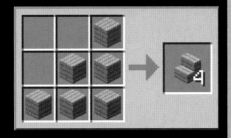

Wool String

You can collect Wool by using Shears on sheep, but if you collect four pieces of string after killing spiders you can also craft a piece of Wool.

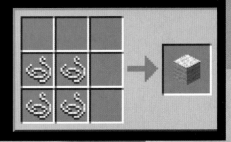

Special trial offer

Enjoyed this book?

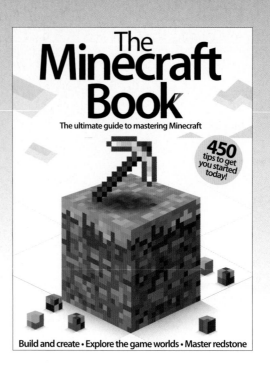

The Minecraft Book

The ultimate guide to mastering Minecraft

450 tips to get you started today!

Build and create · Explore the game worlds · Master redstone

Exclusive offer for new

Try 3 issues for just £5*

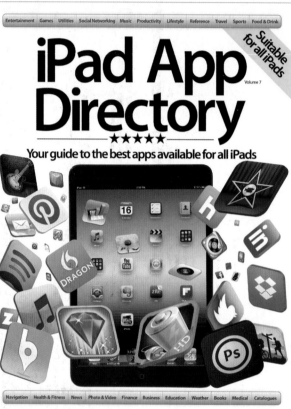